THE PORT OF SILLOTH

1859 – 2009

A PICTORIAL HISTORY THROUGH 150 YEARS OF A SOLWAY PORT

by Capt Chris Puxley

Copy number 17 of a limited edition of 1000 copies.

Foreword

By Captain John Green
Port Manager and Harbour Master
The ABP Ports of Barrow and Silloth - 1988 to 2000

I feel very honoured to have been asked to write the foreword to this book and I should like to congratulate Captain Chris Puxley on his excellent history of the port of Silloth. I am sure that readers with an interest in the port, the town or shipping generally will find it fascinating. As the year 2009 marks the 150th anniversary of the opening of the first dock at Silloth, it is a very appropriate time to look back at what has been achieved over the years. History is important when considering the future, as much can be learned from the successes as well as the misfortunes of the past. It is very gratifying therefore to see the wealth of historical material which has been retained by those with an interest in the port and to recognise all the time and effort that has been put into its compilation. They say that a picture is worth a thousand words and the book certainly exemplifies that old adage.

The port of Silloth's first two owners had been railway companies. That situation changed when the government nationalised the railways in January 1948, bringing it into national ownership. In 1963, Silloth Docks and the other railway ports which were not packet or ferry ports, were separated from railway management and became part of the newly created British Transport Docks Board. The port of Silloth remained in national ownership until the BTDB was privatised and became Associated British Ports Holdings PLC in February 1983.

After 23 years as a PLC, ABPH was then sold into private ownership and removed from the stock market in August 2006.

With all the changes in ownership, methods of cargo transportation and patterns of trade over the years, many of the smaller ports around the country lost their traditional traffics and some ceased to trade commercially. It is very pleasing to see that, despite the fluctuating fortunes of some of Silloth's traffics, the port continues to be successful. This reflects great credit on the efficiency and dedication of the small team who run the port, the stevedoring company and perhaps most importantly the port's customers, especially Carr's Mill, whose loyalty and commitment to the port for over 120 years has been a fundamental contribution to its success.

I first visited Silloth in 1968 and I was delighted, when 20 years later, I was asked to take over responsibility for the port. Despite its modest size, Silloth holds a special place in the hearts of people who have worked in and for the port over the years and I know that I speak for everyone in wishing it continuing success and good fortune in the future.

John Green B.A.
January 2009

*Rubbing of a medal, struck in 1856 to commemorate
the founding of the "Silloth Bay Steam Navigation Co. Ltd."*

Preface

Within Britain's vast maritime history, the small Cumbrian port of Silloth is not particularly old, nor did its form evolve from the benefit of any natural haven or river mouth. The location was chosen because it was a convenient area of undeveloped land within striking distance of Carlisle, sited close to relatively deep water, and was built and opened by enterprising Victorians only 150 years ago, in August 1859.

What else was happening that year? Well, Oregon became the 33rd U.S. State, work began on excavating the Suez Canal, oil was discovered in Titusville, Pennsylvania, Charles Darwin published "The Origin of the Species", the pre-sea training ship HMS *Conway* was established and moored on the Mersey, (of which I am proud to be an Old Boy, 1961-63), and the first ever 'Dog Show' was held in Newcastle on Tyne! For several years now, I have been amassing what is to me, a fascinating collection of photographs, drawings, plans and general information relating to the history of Silloth Docks.

Several people who have seen the collection have remarked that I ought to produce a book, to enable others to enjoy viewing some of the numerous items it contains. It was a task that I had intended to put off until I retired, but then the 150th Anniversary of the opening of the original dock was approaching and so it seemed an appropriate time to grasp the nettle and get on with it.

The resulting content of this book is just a carefully selected sample from that collection, but I hope you will find it interesting and representative of events that have occurred here during the life so far, of this small part of our national maritime heritage, which also just happens to be the most north-westerly port in England.

Acknowledgements

My thanks go to the following, for sharing their memories and giving or allowing me to copy their photographs, documents and plans, not all of which have I been able to include in this small book, but nevertheless are stored within the main collection. They have allowed me to compile a large part of the jigsaw puzzle that is the history of this port. There are still many pieces to find and that must be our joint quest, so that as complete a picture as possible can then be handed on to future generations.

G.Akitt, T.Barker, W.Bisset, G.Bland, A.Brown, N.Dakers, A.Earnshaw, T.Grahamslaw, A.Harrison, E.Hulbert, W.Jameson-Brown, A.Kemp, P.Marr, P.McDowell, K.McCracken, L.McGovarin, P.McRobert, N.Mounsey, P.Ostle, F.Previtali, I.Ramsey, J.Ray, F.Reynolds, M.Scott-Parker, E.Stanwix, R.Straughton, E.Stronach, A.Taylorson, E.Watson, G.Wilkinson, M.Wilson, E.Winter, K.Winter, O.&H.Wood, Associated British Ports, Carrs Milling Industries, Cumberland Newspapers, Cumbria County Archives, Holm St Cuthbert History Group, RNLI (Silloth), Tullie House Museum and especially J.Huggon and S.Wright for their valuable assistance in compiling the main archive. My sincere apologies go to any contributor that I may have inadvertently omitted from this list. Every effort has been made to contact copyright holders of original images in order to obtain permission for reproduction in this book. Again, apologies to anyone who has eluded our efforts.

I thank sponsors and advertisers, and finally, my grateful thanks go the the staff of the Cromwell Press Group for their work in reproducing original material of varying quality and bringing the book to what we hope readers will consider to be a successful conclusion.

Chris Puxley   Silloth   May 2009

Front cover : With Carr's mill in the background, the **Swedica Hav** *leaves Silloth on 16 April 2009 after discharging a cargo of wheat from Rostock.*
(Stephen Wright)

Why Silloth? - An Historical Introduction

Towards the end of the 18th century, the city of Carlisle, which was by far the largest commercial hub in the region, had grown to be a flourishing centre for the spinning and weaving industry, involving the manufacture of cotton goods. This was despite the difficulties encountered in the transport of raw materials and the distribution of the manufactured goods. Roads were poor and the country's railway system was still very much in its infancy. Rail links to the city were non-existent at that time. Transport by water was therefore cheap, extensive and a vital means of commerce, with many of the major towns and cities having waterway connections around the coast and via a growing network of inland canals.

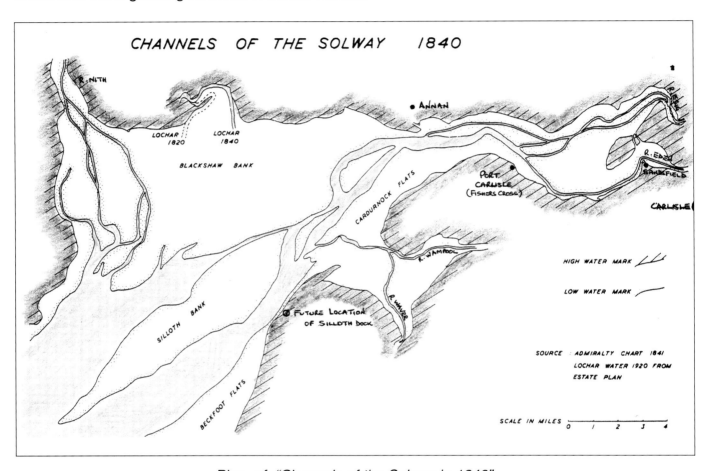

Plan of "Channels of the Solway in 1840".
At this time conditions in the estuary were completely natural. Some later alternations in channel courses can be traced to the construction of Silloth dock (1859), Bowness viaduct (1868) and the controlling of the Nith (begun 1961).

Shipping access to Carlisle was not easy. After arriving safely within the wide outer mouth of the Solway Firth, the ship-master had to then pilot his way for another 30 miles through the shifting, shallow and difficult estuarial channels of the upper Solway Firth, eventually arriving at the mouth of the river Eden. From there the river was only navigable by small vessels and then only as far as Sandsfield, still some five miles from the city. Small seagoing craft such as ketches and schooners were unable to sail up the Solway any further than Fishers Cross, a tiny coastal hamlet that lay eleven miles by rough road from Carlisle. It was there that those vessels had to lay on the foreshore as the tide ebbed, whilst being loaded or discharged by use of a motley collection of horse drawn carts on the exposed beach.

A topsail schooner in the Solway.

These small cargo boats could navigate from sea to the upper Solway Firth, only as far as the beach at Fishers Cross, (later known as Port Carlisle). There they would dry out as the tide ebbed, enabling carts and barrows to be drawn up alongside to load or discharge the cargo.

Samuel Bough's painting of "The Solway Firth at Port Carlisle".
(National Gallery of Scotland)

The burgeoning industry of canal building resulted in the passing of an Act of Parliament in 1819, permitting the formation of The Carlisle Canal Company, who were tasked with building a navigable canal from the coastal hamlet of Fishers Cross to the bustling city of Carlisle. Excavation work began and the canal was completed and officially opened on 12 March 1823. Fishers Cross soon became known as Port Carlisle. This title gave an impression of extensive port facilities, but in fact at the time there was little more to be seen other than a wooden jetty, which dried out at low water, and a sea-lock for the entrance to the canal.

*The opening of the Carlisle Canal 12 March 1823,
as depicted on a Canal Company Share Certificate.*

Trade on the canal initially was brisk, and traffic even included a small but relatively fast horse-drawn passenger boat service between the city and the sea. A couple of small shipping companies were formed locally and commenced a competing service to and from Liverpool, the gateway to the rest of the world. Trade routes were soon introduced to Dublin and Belfast, via the Isle of Man.

*Poster of
The Carlisle &
Liverpool SNCo*

The
Carlisle & Liverpool
Steam Navigation Company

BEG to announce to the Public that in place of the SOLWAY and CUMBERLAND STEAM PACQUETS, which have regularly Plied between LIVERPOOL and PORT CARLISLE, they have brought on the Station the Powerful New Steam Ship

THE NEWCASTLE

JOSEPH SEWELL, COMMANDER

Measuring 396 Tons, Coppered and Copper Fastened, and propelled by Two Engines of Eighty Horse Power each, and is intended to perform Two Voyages weekly between LIVERPOOL and PORT CARLISLE, calling off Whitehaven to land and receive Passengers, and also at Annan Water-foot to land and receive Goods, Live Stock, and Passengers.

Other than improving channel buoyage in the port approaches and the building of a stone jetty, further ambitious plans of enclosed docks and to build a linking canal from Carlisle to Newcastle never materialised. A railway between those cities was approved in 1829, which briefly contributed towards the good fortunes of The Carlisle Canal Company. The news was not all good however. It was becoming clear that the tortuous access and shifting channels and depths of the upper Solway Firth, along with the limitations of the small canal itself, were a considerable restriction to trade expansion.

The "Lees Scar" lighthouse, (also known locally as the "Tommy Legs",
after a Mr Tommy Geddes, one of the early lighthouse keepers).

The "Lees Scar" lighthouse was built and lit in 1841, to mark a 'scar' or outcrop of hard clay, located off Blitterlees, about two miles south-west of Silloth. Built before the dock at Silloth, this offshore beacon served as the front of two leading lights that indicated the line of the Silloth Channel, which was part of the route to and from Port Carlisle. The rear of those two beacons was the "Cote" lighthouse, situated on the shoreline about a mile and a half to the north-east. The light on this "Lees Scar" structure was discontinued in 1938, but then re-established in 1959 after a conveniently located leading light on the end of Silloth Pier was lost as yet another part of the structure collapsed.

*Solway navigation aids for shipping to Port Carlisle. The Solway lightship (right) and **East Cote** (or **Cote**) lighthouse (below).*

By 1840, the existing trade was starting to decline as economical ships became larger. Railway links to Carlisle were improving rapidly although waterborne access was still desirable for long-distance trading. Economic forces eventually prevailed so that on 1 August 1853 the Carlisle Canal was closed to traffic and subsequently drained. A railway track was laid along its length, enabling Port Carlisle to remain open for the time being, but by 1854 the two main shipping companies ceased their operations, ringing the death knell for that maritime venture.

In 1852, during the time of decline at Port Carlisle, a Carlisle industrialist Mr J P Dixon, was proposing the construction of a new purpose-built dock, where ships could remain afloat, to be located a little further down the Solway Firth. He formed a company in order to promote a scheme to build a railway link to Silloth Bay, a virtually uninhabited area consisting of a farming hamlet and coastal sand dunes. The waters offshore had been charted by the Admiralty and were known to be relatively deep close to the shore. This new venture was entitled "The Carlisle & Silloth Bay Railway & Dock Company".

The plan drew considerable opposition, especially from the authorities at Maryport and Workington, however it also attracted influential support from men such as Mr William Marshall, Member of Parliament for the area, and Mr J D Carr, a highly respected Carlisle biscuit manufacturer. In 1853 a prospectus was issued to potential shareholders and by 1854 the scheme was presented to Parliament.

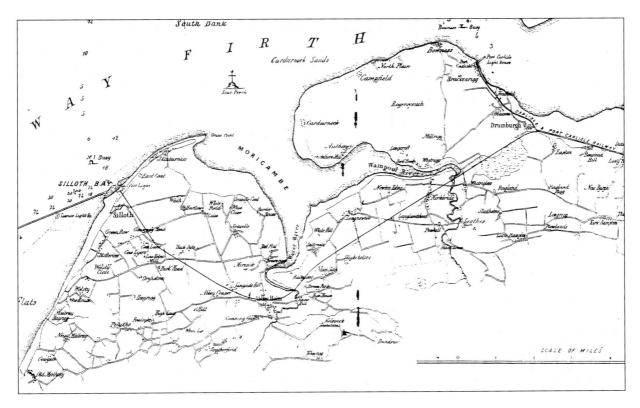

Map of the proposed Silloth branch line, September 1853.

On 16 July 1855 the "Carlisle & Silloth Bay Railway & Dock Act (1855)" was passed, allowing the aforementioned Company to construct their railway branch line to Silloth Bay and there to build a dock. A month later the work on the branch line from Drumburgh began and by 28 August 1856 the track was completed and officially opened.

Poster of the opening of the line ceremony, 28 August 1856.

Also in 1856, work began to build a 1000 feet long timber piled and decked pier on the south side of the proposed dock entrance. The pier was going to be long enough for ships to secure alongside at all states of the tide. At the same time, work began on excavating the dock itself, located behind a massive curved timber cofferdam strengthened with earthworks. This allowed the 600 feet x 300 feet dock to be built partially into the existing sand dunes and partly out into an area reclaimed from the sea by the cofferdam. The dock, enclosing 4 acres of water, was to be built mainly with sandstone blocks from a Dumfriesshire quarry. The entrance would be 60 feet wide and sealed by two pairs of timber-built mitred gates, the outer pair being reverse or sea gates, for protection during stormy weather. The dock gates, cranes and a pair of coal wagon hoists, to be located on the north side of the dock, would all be powered by a fresh water hydraulic system. A depth of 24 feet would be achieved over the entrance sill at ordinary spring tides, whilst the dock itself would be approximately 18 inches deeper.

1856 saw the founding of the Silloth Bay Steam Navigation Company Ltd, as a subsidiary of the Dock & Railway Company. They gained ownership of three vessels and ordered the building of a new screw ship, to be called **Silloth**.

By 1857 the pier was operational and shipping services began to Liverpool, Dublin and Belfast, using the recently-built steam-powered s.s. **Silloth**, along with two other suitable and similar vessels. (Note: The prefix s.s. in those days stood for 'screw ship', as opposed to p.s. for a 'paddle ship').

*Painting of the 154 feet long s.s **Silloth**, built at Port Glasgow by Lawrence Hill & Co. She was sold to Norwegian owners in 1891 and renamed **Storfjord**.*

Engraving of the proposed entrance to Silloth Bay Dock, 1857.

SILLOTH PIER.

The 1000 feet long and 25 feet wide timber-piled pier at Silloth Dock, completed in 1857.

Silloth Lighthouse and Pier

A close-up view of the elegant pagoda-styled pierhead lighthouse.
(For some reason, there appear to be no buffers at the end of the rail track!)
Steps led down to a small landing stage on the south side of the pier.

A supplement to The Carlisle Journal, dated 1857. "View of the Proposed Town of Silloth, and Harbour Works. Now in progress, under the direction of James Abernathy, M.I.C.E."

An early drawing of the earthworks and cofferdam at what will become the entrance to the Silloth Dock. Viewed from the northern side near where the lifeboat station is now located. The pier is completed and the view shows the Scottish hills across the Solway.

With excavation work well underway a ceremonial laying of the dock foundation stone in the north-east corner of the dock was carried out by Sir James Graham on 18 August 1857, attracting an estimated crowd of five thousand people. A timber box was placed beneath the stone, containing coins of the realm, newspapers of the day, a dock prospectus, along with plans and views of the proposed town and dock at Silloth.

As the next couple of years passed by, housing, shops and hotels, served by wide cobbled roads and other facilities gradually began to develop to a grid plan on the north side of the dock construction area, all of which would eventually grow into the new town of Silloth-on-Solway.

18 August 1857.
Engraving of the laying of the Silloth Bay Dock foundation stone,

On 3 August 1859, the Silloth Bay Dock was officially opened with due ceremony. A public holiday was declared at Carlisle and special trains were laid on to carry passengers to Silloth for the occasion. The s.s. **Silloth**, suitably decorated with flags and bunting and escorted by several other vessels, embarked dignitaries then sailed from her berth at Silloth pier and into the Solway Firth. At the signal of a gun being fired, she sailed back and entered the dock with her escorts. During the following ceremony, the Chairman of the Dock Company officially declared that the dock be named "Marshall Dock", (after Mr William Marshall, the MP for East Cumberland), and that it was now open to shipping. The total cost of works to establish the dock and pier at Silloth Bay had amounted to £122,000.

Engraving of the opening of Marshall Dock, 3 August 1859.

The Early Silloth Lifeboats (1860 – 1896)

On 25 June 1860, a lifeboat station for the Royal National Lifeboat Institution was opened at Silloth, located immediately north of the Marshall Dock entrance. During August of the previous year, there was a near tragedy in the Solway Firth, when the schooner **Mary**, carrying a cargo of slate up the estuary to Port Carlisle, ran aground on the Silloth Bank in a storm. The crew of four were very close to death when they were luckily spotted and rescued by the passing steamer **Queen**, of Dumfries. The **Mary** and her cargo were a total loss.

Although by no means the first such incident in these waters, this event raised public awareness of the dangers to seafarers in the Solway and a subscription list was started in Carlisle to buy a lifeboat. A local philanthropist, Miss Burdett-Coutts, offered to buy the lifeboat if others subscribers would supply the boathouse and fund the maintenance of the station. The Appeal was a success and the "Opening Day" was recorded in the national periodical "Illustrated Times" on 14 July 1860.

Engraving of "Launch of a lifeboat at Silloth", that accompanied an article in the "Illustrated Times" dated 14 July 1860.

The first Silloth lifeboat was named **Angela and Hannah**, after Miss Burdett-Coutts and her sister. Built by Forrest & Son of Limehouse, London, it was of a self-righting design, 30 feet long, propelled by oars and sails and initially had a crew of eight, later increased to ten. This lifeboat remained on station until replaced in 1867.

The second lifeboat to be stationed at Silloth was a similar self-righting craft, again named **Angela and Hannah**, but two feet longer and manned by a crew of thirteen. It was not long on station when it had to be launched in rough seas on 10 October 1868, to a fishing smack in distress. On reaching the swamped boat, no life was found. Turning eastwards and following a line of debris from the wreck, they came upon the sole surviving occupant of the **Rover**, clinging to pieces of wood. James Rae was rescued and brought back to Silloth Dock. Eight other service launches were recorded saving a total of seven lives.

Angela & Hannah (II) (1867 – 1877).

In 1877, the **Angela and Hannah** was renamed **Mary Louisa**, after Miss Mary Browne of Liverpool, who left a legacy to maintain the lifeboat, which continued to guard the upper Solway until relieved in 1885.

The third RNLI lifeboat at Silloth was the **Emma Frisby**, a 34 feet long improved version of her predecessor. She arrived on station on 11 March 1885, as a gift to the RNLI from Miss Annie F Howis, of London. All these early lifeboats were normally carriage launched from the beach, a laborious and difficult process involving the gathering of a team of horses and men to haul the boat and carriage to the water's edge.

*The Silloth lifeboat **Emma Frisby** (1885 – 1896).*

During the long winter months, the Silloth lifeboats were often left afloat in the Marshall Dock, which became tidal in 1879. In 1895, the coxswain registered his concern that the lifeboat was only afloat for five hours out of every twelve, a very unsatisfactory situation for a rescue service. Consequently, the District Inspector of Lifeboats recommended that the station be closed, but the local Lifeboat Committee disagreed, wanting to maintain whatever service was possible. The Chief Inspector of Lifeboats eventually stepped in and reluctantly closed Silloth Lifeboat Station on 13 August 1896. The nearest Lifeboat Station now was located at Maryport, opened in 1865 but a good distance from the treacherous upper Solway Firth. Mariners in distress in this area would now have to rely on fellow seafarers for assistance.

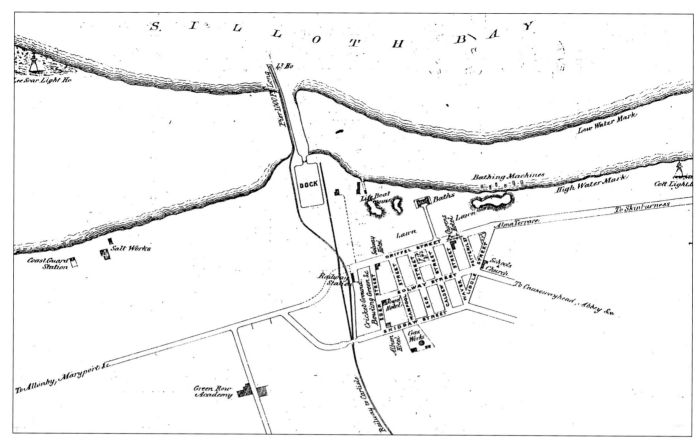

Lonsdale's Plan of Silloth, 1860.

With the opening of the Marshall Dock at Silloth, traffic volume through the port was initially slow to build up, so to make it more attractive, ship dues were increased at Port Carlisle and several navigation aids were discontinued upstream of Silloth Dock. Cross-Solway services from Silloth were introduced to Annan and Dumfries, in addition to the existing services to Liverpool, Dublin and Belfast. The cross-Solway shipping services gradually became unviable due to the construction of a railway viaduct across the Firth from Bowness-on-Solway to Annan, and were terminated in 1878.

*The **Carham**, employed on cross-Solway services 1864-1867.*

The Marshall Dock, showing warehousing and the two gantries, known as coal-hoists, for lifting coal wagons and tipping their contents into ships' holds.

Diagram of the workings of the early coal-hoists located on the north side of Marshall Dock.

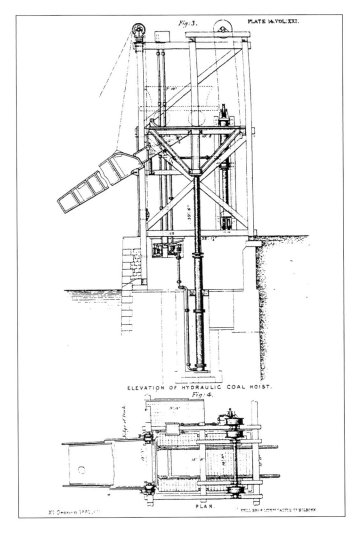

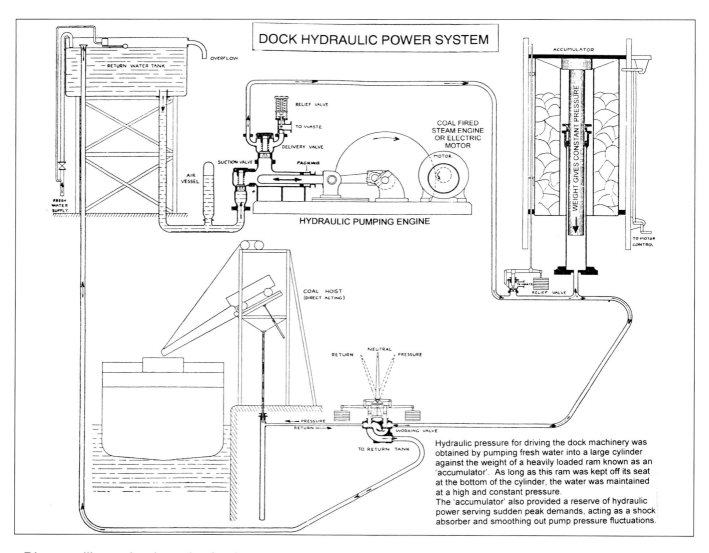

DOCK HYDRAULIC POWER SYSTEM

RETURN WATER TANK

OVERFLOW

RELIEF VALVE

TO WASTE

DELIVERY VALVE

COAL FIRED
STEAM ENGINE
OR ELECTRIC
MOTOR

MOTOR.

AIR
VESSEL

SUCTION VALVE

PACKING

FRESH
WATER
SUPPLY.

HYDRAULIC PUMPING ENGINE

ACCUMULATOR

WEIGHT GIVES CONSTANT PRESSURE

TO MOTOR
CONTROL

RELIEF VALVE

COAL HOIST
(DIRECT ACTING)

RETURN   NEUTRAL   PRESSURE

PRESSURE

RETURN

WORKING VALVE

TO RETURN TANK

Hydraulic pressure for driving the dock machinery was
obtained by pumping fresh water into a large cylinder
against the weight of a heavily loaded ram known as an
'accumulator'. As long as this ram was kept off its seat
at the bottom of the cylinder, the water was maintained
at a high and constant pressure.
The 'accumulator' also provided a reserve of hydraulic
power serving sudden peak demands, acting as a shock
absorber and smoothing out pump pressure fluctuations.

*Diagram illustrating how the fresh water hydraulic system worked and powered the coal wagon hoists,
cranes and dock gate machinery. The water tank, pump machinery and accumulator were housed
in a building on the north side of Marshall Dock.*

*The hydraulic pump and accumulator house,
with shrimp fishing boats in Marshall Dock in the foreground.*

By 1862, the Carlisle & Silloth Bay Railway & Dock Company was in financial difficulties due to a breakdown of trust between itself and the Newcastle & Carlisle Railway Company, which had reneged on a promise to provide trade from their network. The North British Railway Company then took over the ownership and operation of the Silloth branch line and the dock, along with the Silloth Bay Steam Navigation Company, which they renamed The North British Steam Packet Company.

Silloth Dock and shipping, 1867.

In 1873, William Crabb opened "The Border Counties Chemical & Manure Works" at Silloth and would have relied heavily on imports of raw materials imported through the dock. This business was taken over by Messrs Graham, Maxwell & Farlie in 1879, who renamed it the "Solway Chemical Works". Sometime later, the business partners Graham and Farlie relinquished their interests and the factory became known as "Maxwell's Chemical Works". Around 1950, the chemical works was taken over by Fison's, who expanded the business but eventually the facility failed to be profitable and closed down in the mid-1960s.

Advertisement for William Crabb's Chemical Works.

WILLIAM CRABB,

THE BORDER COUNTIES

Chemical & Manure Works,

SILLOTH, CUMBERLAND.

MANUFACTURER OF

SULPHURIC ACID

AND

ARTIFICIAL MANURES

FOR ALL CROPS.

Bones, Bone Meal, Coprolites and other Phosphates.

Guano, Sulphate of Ammonia, Potash, Kainit, &c.

On afternoon of 6 April 1879, catastrophe struck! During a storm and following a spate of winter gales, the entrance walls of Marshall Dock and the dock gates collapsed, probably due to a gradual undermining and weakening of these exposed man-made structures by the erosive force of the wind and waves. The dock quickly drained, trapping and grounding a large number of vessels inside. It took almost two weeks for the combined efforts of the resident paddle tug **Arabian** and dockside locomotives to clear the debris sufficiently to release the trapped vessels.

Marshall Dock entrance collapse, 6 April 1879.

A "Notice of Protest" letter from the captain of the barque **Treci Dubrovachi**, is one of several from trapped vessels and all registered against the owner of the dock, the North British Railway Company, for damage to their craft, following the collapse of Marshall Dock entrance on 6 April 1879.

The letter states:

"He arrived in Silloth Roads on the 29th of March last and anchored there. That he entered the Dock at Silloth on the 4th of April instant and commenced to discharge his cargo at 1 p.m. On the 6th of April, at about 4.30 p.m. when the tide was out, the Dock Gates and part of the Dock Wall gave way. The water rushed out of the Dock and a few minutes afterwards his Barque was left aground on her beam ends (on her side). That she is in a dangerous position straining greatly and has already started a leak, which is increasing and although the pumps are left constantly at work the water is increasing and damaging the cargo. The entrance of the Dock is owing to the above circumstances blocked up and there is no means of getting in or out.

That from the above circumstances loss and damage is incurred and he therefore enters his Protest against the North British Railway Company the Proprietors and Lessees of the Marshall Dock, Silloth and all whom it may concern and holds them liable for all damage and losses incurred already and which may be hereafter incurred arising from the said circumstances".

Treci Dubrovachi

At **Carlisle**
the **seventh** day of **April** 18**79**
Before **Robert Heysham Mounsey**
Notary Public duly authorised and practising at the
City of Carlisle

Appeared personally **Matteo Turcinovich**
Captain of the **Barque** **Treci Dubrovachi**
belonging to **the Port of Ragusa in Austria**
583 Tons Register and stated that he arrived in Silloth Roads on the 29ᵗʰ of March last and anchored there That he entered the Dock at Silloth on the 4ᵗʰ of April instant and commenced to discharge his cargo at 1 p m On the 5ᵗʰ of April about 4.30 p m when the tide was out the Dock Gates and front of the Dock Wall gave way the Water rushed out of the Dock and a few minutes afterwards his Barque was left aground on her beam ends That she is in a dangerous position straining greatly and has already started a Leak which is increasing and though the Pumps are kept constantly at work the water is increasing and damaging the Cargo The entrance of the Dock is owing to the above circumstances blocked up and there is no means of getting in or out

~~loss and~~

That from the above circumstances ~~he fears~~ loss and damage is incurred and he therefore enters his Protest against the North British Railway Company the Proprietors and Lessees of the Marshall Dock Silloth and all whom it may concern and holds them liable for all damages and losses incurred already and ~~therefore enters his Protest~~ which may be hereafter incurred arising from the said circumstances

Matteo Turcinovich

In the presence of
R. H. Mounsey
Notary Public

Photocopy of the actual letter.

By June 1879, temporary repairs to the entrance walls were completed, allowing full shipping services to return to Silloth and the dock, although the dock gates were never reinstated and Marshall Dock remains a tidal basin to the present day.

In May 1882, the North British Railway Company commenced work on the construction of a second dock, immediately inland from the Marshall Dock and consequently better sheltered from the effects of rough seas. This new dock, when completed, would encompass a water area of 6 acres, be 400 feet wide, with a length of 630 feet on the northern wall and 660 feet on the southern wall. The additional length on the southern wall would allow for a temporary timber cofferdam to be inserted at the eastern end, which could be broken through if there was a demand at some later date to extend the dock system and provide increased quay capacity. The 36 feet high dock walls were built of very strong concrete, topped with granite cope-stones, quarried at Dalbeattie, Shap and Cornwall. The entrance to this new dock would be 125 feet long and 60 feet wide, having a granite base laid on thick concrete. A pair of greenheart timber mitre gates, each weighing 70 tons, would retain 24 feet of water over the entrance sill at ordinary spring tides, with 26 feet of water in the dock itself. The dock gates, along with several quayside cranes and a new coal-wagon hoist would be powered by a new fresh water hydraulic ring main, linked to the existing pumping station on the north side of Marshall Dock. Four large mooring buoys would be moored within the dock to supplement numerous quayside bollards and assist with warping ships around the dock. During the excavation of this second dock, various mammalian fossils were uncovered including red deer antlers, skeletal parts of a gigantic ox and the vertebrae of a whale.

Silloth second dock, or New Dock under construction, 1883.

On 30 June 1885 the second, or New Dock, as it became known, was officially opened. The total cost of building the New Dock and associated works had amounted to £90,000. Passing from the Solway Firth and through the Marshall Dock, the first vessel to enter was once again the steamship *Silloth*, breaking a blue ribbon as she entered the New Dock, followed by several other vessels including the s.s. *Albatross*, which was used on the Silloth - Liverpool service. A VIP lunch was held at the Queen's Hotel and workers were later served a "knife and fork tea". This was followed by an evening of sports and entertainment on a field by the railway station.

Albatross entering the New Dock for the first time, 30 June 1885.

In 1886, the old Silloth paddle tug **Arabian** was sold and replaced by the **Solway** which is seen lying in New Dock alongside the Solway lightship.

In 1887, the biscuit manufacturer Carr & Co. of Carlisle built and opened a new 'fireproof steam flour mill' alongside the New Dock, to which ships sailing from as far away as Australia and America came to discharge their cargoes of grain.

Drawings of Carr's flour mill, built 1887.

*An unidentified paddle tug towing a barque out of the New Dock,
with the recently completed Carr's flour mill behind, c 1890s.*

*Extract from a North British Railway's poster c. late 1880s,
depicting the port of Silloth and including the New Dock.*

*11 July 1892. The sailing ship **Royal George**, from Melbourne after a normal four-month voyage, with a cargo of Australian wheat, entering Silloth Docks led by the paddle tug **Solway** and assisted by another unidentified twin-funnelled paddle tug.*

Ship's masters are obliged to "Note Protest" if on their voyage they experienced heavy weather or other incident, causing possible or real damage to ship or cargo.

"At Carlisle on 11th July 1892, before Anthony Nichol Bowman, Notary Public duly authorised and practicing at the City of Carlisle.

*Appearing personally Alexander Foggart, Captain of the ship **Royal George**, belonging to the port of Liverpool, 1404 Tons Register and stated that he sailed from Melbourne on 2nd March last, laden with a cargo of wheat consigned to Messrs Carr & Co, Silloth. That he encountered severe gales during the first part of the voyage and shipped a good deal of water, one of the ship's boats being smashed. That he arrived at Silloth on Sunday the 10th inst. about 11 a.m. and entered the Docks at 2 p.m. on Monday 11th inst.*

That from the above circumstances he fears damage to his ship and cargo and therefore enters his Protest.

Alexander Foggart

In the presence of A.N. Bowman, Notary Public."

*A "Note of Protest" from the captain of the **Royal George**, 11 July 1892.*

24 August 1892.
*The s.s. **Vulcan** lying on the south side of New Dock with a cargo of phosphate rock from Coosaw, South Carolina. The cargo is probably consigned to the chemical works at Silloth.*

"At Carlisle on 24th August 1892, before Anthony Nichol Bowman, Notary Public duly authorised and practicing in the City of Carlisle.

*Appeared personally Joseph Edmondson, Captain of the s.s. **Vulcan**, belonging to West Hartlepool 1441 Tons Register and stated that he sailed from Coosaw, S. Carolina on the 5th August bound for Silloth, laden with a cargo of phosphate rock consigned to order.*

That at different times during the passage he experienced very stormy and tempestuous weather, shipping a great quantity of seas all over the vessel. That he arrived off Silloth and in entering the Dock on the 24th the steamer took the ground and stranded and came off again and entered the Dock at 1 p.m. in the afternoon of the same day.

That from the above circumstances he fears damage to his ship and cargo and therefore enters his Protest.

Jos. Edmondson

In the presence of A.N. Bowman, Notary Public."

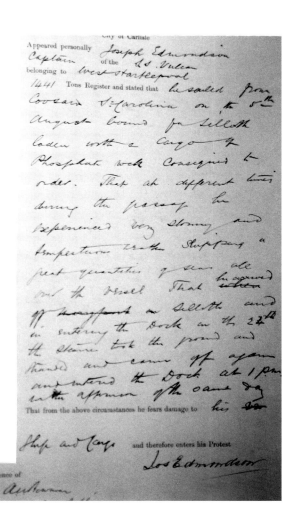

*A "Note of Protest" from the captain of the s.s. **Vulcan**.*

An early steamship, still equipped with sails, alongside Carr's mill – c. 1890s.

1893 saw the introduction of what would become a long-serving vessel at Silloth. Built by R. Napier & Sons of Glasgow and launched in June of that year, she was the new iron-built screw steamer **Yarrow**, belonging to William Sloan & Co. of Glasgow. Of 972 gross registered tons, later reduced to 959 grt, she was 230 feet long, 32 feet 1 inch beam and had a loaded draught of 15 feet. Powered by a triple expansion compound steam engine of 223 horse power, she managed 13 knots. The **Yarrow** commenced a twice-weekly service to Dublin via the Isle of Man. Advertised as being lit by electricity, she carried passengers, general freight and livestock.

*The s.s. **Yarrow**, which commenced services from Silloth to Dublin via the Isle of Man, from 1893 to 1943.*

Yarrow timetables

In addition to the **Yarrow**, the two other regular callers at Silloth were the s.s. **Albatross** and the s.s. **Kittiwake**, both owned by the North British Steam Packet Company. The two ships maintained in tandem, a freight and passenger service between Silloth and Liverpool, right up until the end of the First World War.

The **Kittiwake** entering Silloth Docks.

One of the largest ships ever to enter Silloth was the s.s. **Aggi**, which arrived on 8 January 1897 with a part cargo of wheat from San Francisco. The **Aggi** was 103 metres in length and must have been a cumbersome vessel to bring into the New Dock in those days. This vessel, seen alongside Carr's mill, is believed to be the **Aggi**.

Crowds attend the departure of this unidentified but attractive steam yacht, c. 1890s. The grand vessel could be connected with the Shahzda of Afghanistan who represented his nephew King Amanullah on a visit in June 1895 to see guns being tested at the W G Armstrong testing battery located a mile south of Silloth Docks (see map on page 32).

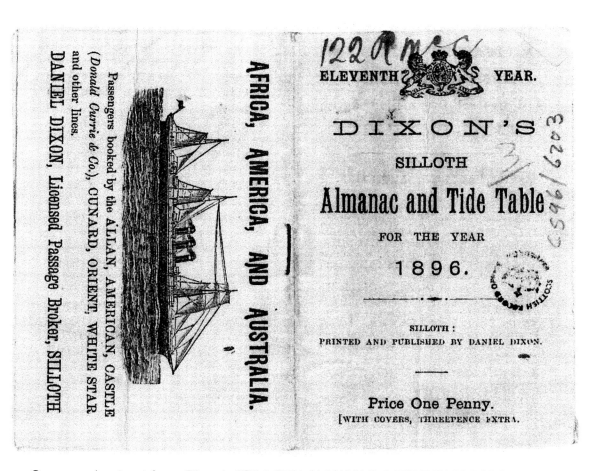

*Cover and extract from Dixon's "SILLOTH ALMANAC & TIDE TABLES" for 1896.
Daniel Dixon had been producing these useful little booklets
at Silloth since 1885, costing just one penny..*

APARTMENTS TO LET AT SILLOTH.

Mrs. SMITH, 3 Marine Terrace—1 Dining, Drawing, and Breakfast Room, 6 Bedrooms, 1 Bath Room.

Miss CARRUTHERS, 13 Caldew Street—2 Sitting Rooms, 5 Bedrooms.

Mrs. HARRISON, 11 Caldew Street—1 Sitting Room, 3 Bedrooms.

Mrs. HUGHES, 2 Marine Terrace—1 Dining Drawing, and Breakfast Room, 6 Bedrooms, 1 Bath Room.

Mrs. JOHNSTONE, Liddle Terrace—1 Sitting Room, 3 Bedrooms.

Mrs. KAYE, 4 Criffel Street—2 Sitting Rooms, 4 Bedrooms.

Mrs. MAKIN, 9 Caldew Street—1 Sitting Room, 3 Bedrooms.

Miss PEARSON, 15 Caldew Street—2 Sitting Rooms, 5 Bedrooms.

Miss RIDDLE, 4 Marine Terrace—1 Dining, Drawing, and Breakfast Room, 6 Bedrooms, 1 Bath Room.

JANUARY.

Day		Morn H M	H'ight FT IN	Even H M	H'ight FT IN
1 W	....	...	...	0 7	22 6
2 Th	....	0 28	22 6	0 50	23 4
3 F	....	1 13	23 3	1 34	24 0
4 S	....	1 57	23 6	2 20	24 2
5 S	....	2 43	23 6	3 7	23 11
6 M	....	3 31	23 2	3 57	23 4
7 T	....	4 23	22 4	4 49	22 4
8 W	....	5 18	21 4	5 48	21 1
9 Th	....	6 21	20 1	6 54	20 1
10 F	....	7 32	19 9	8 9	19 1
11 S	....	8 45	19 6	9 21	19 3
12 S	....	9 53	20 0	10 22	19 10
13 M	....	10 49	20 9	11 13	20 6
14 T	....	11 36	21 6	11 58	21 2
15 W	....	...	...	0 17	22 2
16 Th	....	0 36	21 7	2 38	22 6
17 F	....	1 13	21 10	1 31	22 7
18 S	....	1 48	21 10	2 4	22 5
19 S	....	2 22	21. 7	2 38	22 0
20 M	....	2 55	21 0	3 12	21 3
21 T	....	3 30	20 3	3 48	20 4
22 W	....	4 7	19 4	4 27	19 4
23 Th	....	4 49	18 3	5 15	18 3
24 F	....	5 43	17 5	6 15	17 5
25 S	....	6 50	16 9	7 39	16 8
26 S	....	8 8	17 3	8 46	17 2
27 M	....	9 20	18 1	9 51	18 4
28 T	....	10 18	19 7	10 44	19 11
29 W	....	11 8	21 4	11 30	21 7
30 Th	....	11 53	23 2	...	...
31 F	....	0 16	23 3	0 38	24 9

1901 Ordnance Survey map of Silloth and the Docks.

On 28 June 1905, Carr's flour mill formally reopened to full and increased output, following a year of major building expansion, refurbishment and the introduction of new machinery, during which flour production was temporarily reduced.

WHERE THE FAMOUS **CC** FLOUR COMES FROM

CARR & CO'S SOLWAY MILLS, SILLOTH, NEAR CARLISLE

A postcard of Carr's mill showing modifications with an extra floor,
pitched roofs and a new grain elevator. Compare this view with that of 1887.

*The sailing ship **Nerelde** at Carr's mill, discharging wheat from Portland, Oregon, 31 March 1907.*
(Note: A 'ship' carries square sails on 3 or more masts, whilst a 'barque'
has only fore & aft sails on her mizzen mast).

*Two views of the paddle tug **Petrel** (1893-1943)*

This important workhorse was owned by the North British Steam Packet Company, and from 1920 by the North British Railway Company. She and her predecessors at the port of Silloth (the **Arabian** and the **Solway**), were used for numerous tasks. In addition to the obvious duty of assisting shipping in and out of the docks, the resident paddle-tug was also used to tow dredging barges out to sea for dumping, crew changes on the Solway lightship, laying attending to and recovering navigation buoys, towing small becalmed sailing vessels between Solway ports, or larger sailing vessels in from or out past St Bees Head and the open sea.

On 21 June 1907, the s.s. **Ailsa** grounded on a sandbank as she was arriving with a
cargo of Swedish timber. She was stranded there for one tide, blocking
the entrance and preventing the **Yarrow** from entering.
Passengers from the **Yarrow** had to be ferried ashore by using the paddle tug **Petrel**.

24 June 1907.
The whaleback Belgian steamer **Sagamore**, with wheat from Braila, Romania. The unusual oval
hull design was intended to allow seas to wash over the deck without causing damage.
Sagamore would later be captured by a German submarine off Spain in 1917 and sunk.
(Note: the **Ailsa** berthed astern).

Silloth Dock and Carr's Mill.

c. early 1900s. A three-masted barque lying at the coaling berth.

c. early 1900s. A small steam coaster loading a cargo of coal.

A Silloth postcard, stamped 4 August 1908.

*The Norwegian four-masted barque **L'Avenir** at Carr's mill.*

This large vessel called twice at Silloth. Firstly on 13 April 1911 and again on 3 April 1912, both times with wheat from Australia. Built in 1911 for Gustav Erikson, she became the first large sailing vessel to be fitted with a radio transmitter. She sadly disappeared without trace in March 1938.

1911 was a difficult year for Silloth Docks. On the evening of 1 July, the Dock Master met the Lees Scar lighthouse keeper in town, when he should have been manning his lighthouse. To make matters worse, the lighthouse keeper was drunk. Suspending him from duty, he arranged for a deputy to take his place. When the deputy went to take up his duties at about 8.30 pm, he found that the lighthouse was on fire. The blaze had been spotted by others, some of whom reported seeing a figure running away from the scene. The regular keeper was later arrested and sent for trial at Carlisle Assizes, where he was found guilty of having feloniously set the lighthouse on fire. Emergency lights were rigged until the structure was repaired.

1 July 1911. Lees Scar lighthouse on fire.

On Monday 14 August 1911, Silloth's dock workers went on strike. During that month, transport and industrial workers throughout the country were taking action over low wages. As the North British Railway Company refused to increase their pay, the Silloth dockers, amounting to more than 80 men, refused to work. The s.s. **Albatross** lay in port fully laden along with two other vessels. By Thursday, Carr's mill was forced to shut down as grain was not being discharged from vessels. The mill manager reasoned with the dockers but to no avail. At the end of that week a fourth vessel arrived, the **Ardnagrena**, carrying maize for the mill. Carr's manager was forced to take extraordinary measures and ordered his 14 clerical staff to unload the ship, which they did, led by the manager himself and accompanied by police in case of any trouble. No problems arose and the ship was discharged, although taking rather longer than would normally have been the case. The strike ended on 1 September, but it is not known whether the dock workers got an increase in pay.

Note: At this time grain was discharged by hand from the ship's hold, shovelled into large buckets and craned into the mill. It was not until 1913, that the mill acquired a twin-piped suction discharging system.

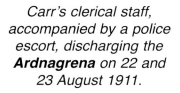

*Carr's clerical staff, accompanied by a police escort, discharging the **Ardnagrena** on 22 and 23 August 1911.*

*The paddle tug **Petrel** was frequently employed towing smaller sailing vessels and their cargoes between Silloth and other Solway ports such as Annan, Glencaple and Carsethorn.*

Leaving the Docks, **Silloth.**

The Schooner *Minnie Coles* Incident - 1912

Extract from the minutes of the monthly management meeting of "The North British Steam Packet Company", (owners of the paddle tug *Petrel*), held in Edinburgh on 9 January 1913:

*"Tug **Petrel** ……. It was reported that on 24th December, (1912), while Tug **Petrel** was towing schooner "Minnie Coles" from Annan to Silloth, she was caught in a heavy gale. The tow rope parted, and the master of the tug was obliged to make for Silloth for shelter and leave the schooner in the Firth; that the captain of the schooner dropped his anchors, but while the vessel held for a time, she was ultimately driven ashore by the gale east of Cote Light, Silloth at 9 pm the same day."*

Extract from the minutes of the monthly management meeting of "The North British Steam Packet Company", held in Edinburgh on 6 February 1913:

*"Tug **Petrel**…… The Secretary submitted a letter from the owner of schooner **Minnie Coles**, claiming damages for failure of tug to go to the rescue of the **Minnie Coles** after the tow rope had parted during hurricane on 24th December last."*

Unfortunately, there is no indication in later minutes of the management meetings as to whether any compensation payment was made to the owner of the **Minnie Coles**, William E Jones, of Glan Menai, Port Dinorwic. The schooner had been built at Port Dinorwic in 1867.

The schooner **Minnie Coles**, which was driven ashore by strong winds
at Skinburness, (just north of Silloth), on 24 December 1912.
Reportedly she was never refloated and was broken up where she lay.

June 1914.
Transferring bagged grain from the barque **Lota** and emptying the bags into the hold of the steam coaster **Agnes Ellen**. The **Lota** had brought 2,200 tons of grain for Carr's flour mill from Fremantle, Australia. On arrival at the Solway Firth she had to anchor off Maryport to discharge approximately 700 tons into the **Agnes Ellen** to reduce her draught sufficiently to be able to enter Silloth on 21 June.

The **Lota** and **Agnes Ellen** alongside Carr's mill, as the **Yarrow** arrives from Dublin.
The old wooden Solway lightship is seen laid up on the western wall.
Of 284 gross registered tons, the **Agnes Ellen** had been built in 1908 and was owned by
James Henry Monks (Preston) Ltd, of Liverpool.

14 June 1912.
*The barque **Dagny** from Sydney, Australia,*
*entering Silloth and towed by the resident paddle tug **Petrel**.*

March 1915.
*The departure of the barque **Fahrwohl**, the very last large commercial sailing vessel to call at Silloth.*

*Two views of the **Yarrow** departing from Silloth, with a crows nest and searchlight on the foremast. It was not removed until the early 1930s.*

During the First World War, the **Yarrow** continued her regular crossing of the Irish Sea to Dublin via the Isle of Man, having been equipped with a searchlight on her foremast, possibly to assist with manoeuvring in confined waters during blackout conditions or to search for and dazzle enemy submarines, which were known to operate in these waters.

Sailings of the **Kittiwake** and **Albatross** to and from Liverpool were suspended on occasions when submarine activity was reported in the area. Later during the war, the **Kittiwake** was commandeered by the Admiralty for Government service on the east coast of England. In 1919, the **Kittiwake** was returned to her owners but then sold and never resumed her Silloth service. The **Albatross** was laid up at Silloth for a while due to lack of business, before being sold, thus ending the long-standing Silloth – Liverpool service.

*The **Albatross** seen sailing from Silloth to Liverpool. She was driven ashore during a gale in December 1894. She grounded off Silloth Baths, north of the dock entrance, (the white building at the left of the photograph). After several attempts during high tides, with tug assistance and some excavation of the beach around her, the **Albatross** was finally refloated on 10 February 1895, after which she was towed to Liverpool for repairs to her rudder.*

In 1920, the assets of the North British Steam Packet Company, which had recently sold its ships **Kittiwake** and **Albatross**, were absorbed back into the North British Railway Company, its only remaining vessel now being the paddle tug **Petrel**.

At some time around 1920, the end of Silloth's 1000 feet long pier began to subside. This was the beginning of the gradual demise for this popular structure, which must have been a wonderful promenade for the general public, affording a fine view of their town from the sea and of ships coming and going at the docks.

*The public on Silloth Pier, with the **Yarrow** arriving and the raised signal ball indicating permission for her to enter the docks. Note the subsidence at the far end of the pier.*

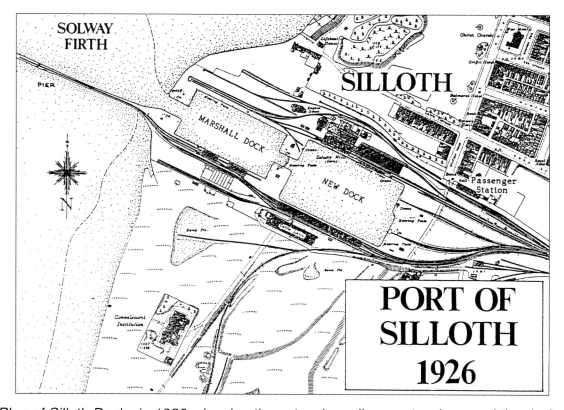

Plan of Silloth Docks in 1926, showing the extensive railway network around the docks.

Probably from well before the port was first built, there have been local fishermen who eked a living from the tidal waters of the Solway Firth. The brown shrimp are numerous in the sandy channels, whilst cockle and mussel beds abound both on the accessible inter-tidal banks and in deeper water. Salmon run to the rivers that flow into the estuary and codling, flatties, eels and sea-bass can be caught on the hook. The arrival of a dock gave those Solway fishermen with boats, an ideal sheltered mooring from the worst of the weather.

A Silloth shrimp boat c.1920s.

*Dating from the same period, the shrimp boat **Foam** belonged to Jim Baxter.*

During the summer months, the fishermen sought and caught larger and more lucrative prey, taking holidaymakers for "trips around the bay". They even built a small landing stage just to the north of the dock, to enable their passengers to board without getting their feet wet.

Two views of Silloth shrimp boats and tourists thought to be in the 1920s.

A local cartoon postcard c.1920s.

The old wooden *Solway* lightship was sold for scrap in 1926. Originally built and placed on station off Dubmill Point in 1840 to mark the entrance of the navigable channel into the upper reaches of the Firth, she was taken out of service when replaced in 1895 by an iron lightship called **Tobin** purchased from the Mersey Docks & Harbour Board. The **Tobin** remained on station off Dubmill Point until 1920, when sold and was replaced by a navigation buoy.

*The iron built lightship **Tobin** with the identifying word **Solway** written on her side. Seen here in Marshall Dock and dressed overall to celebrate the re-opening of Carr's mill in June 1905.*

The old wooden lightship lay in the New Dock until 1926. Her new owner then beached the craft just north of Silloth to recover the copper sheathing from her hull, also cleverly using her as a tearoom, (presumably whilst the tide was out), until broken up in 1929. Her fog bell was donated to Silloth Golf Club but was later stolen and has never been recovered.

The old wooden Solway lightship lies beached to the north of the town, and used as a tearoom, 1926-1929.

In 1929, William Sloan & Co. of Glasgow, owners of the regular Silloth visitor, **Yarrow**, sold its vessel to the Dublin & Silloth Steamship Co. and the ship was initially managed by Palgrave Murphy Ltd of Dublin. The **Yarrow** was renamed **Assaroe**, after Assaroe Abbey, now the remains of a Cistercian foundation of the 12th century, located near Ballyshannon, County Donegal. The Dublin & Silloth Steamship Co. was later acquired by Palgrave Murphy Ltd.

The **Asseroe** continued on her regular twice-weekly service to Douglas and Dublin until the outbreak of the Second World War in 1939. She then maintained a freight only service until her final departure on 21 October 1943.

*The **Assaroe** departing from Silloth to Dublin.*

*Young Norman Dakers of Carlisle, at the wheel of the **Assaroe**.*

SAILINGS FROM SILLOTH.

S.S. "ASSAROE"
carrying Passengers and Cargo

Sails every TUESDAY and SATURDAY
from SILLOTH to

DOUGLAS I.O.M. and DUBLIN

And from Dublin to Silloth every Monday and Thursday
calling at Douglas

SINGLE AND DOUBLE BERTHS.

FULL PASSENGER LICENCE AND WIRELESS.

Particulars from Station Master, Silloth.   (Phone 17).
John Metcalfe, 2, Fort Street, Douglas; or from

PALGRAVE MURPHY, LTD.
17, Eden Quay, DUBLIN.
(Managers for Dublin & Silloth Steamship Co., Ltd.)

N.B.—During Winter Months Steamer calls once weekly at Douglas.

*A poster for the sailings of the **Assaroe**.*

Dublin & Silloth Steamship Co., Ltd.
(PALGRAVE MURPHY LTD.)

☞ Passengers, Passengers' Luggage, Live Stock, and Goods are carried by the Owners of these Steamers, subject to the Conditions on the other side, which are of the essence of the contract.

MAY AND JUNE, 1929.

A timetable and fares for sailings in May and June 1929

DUBLIN TO DOUGLAS

MAY.		JUNE.	
Thurs. 2 at 3- 0 p.m.	Mon. 3 at 6- 0 p.m.
Mon. 6 at 6- 0 p.m.	Thurs. 6 at 8- 0 p.m.
Thurs. 9 at 8- 0 p.m.	Mon. 10 at 10- 0 p.m.
Mon. 13 at 10- 0 p.m.	Thurs. 13 at 2- 0 p.m.
Thurs. 16 at 4-30 p.m.	Mon. 17 at 6- 0 p.m.
Mon. 20 at 7- 0 p.m.	Thurs. 20 at 8- 0 p.m.
Thurs. 23 at 8- 0 p.m.	Mon. 24 at 10- 0 p.m.
Mon. 27 at 10- 0 p.m.	Thurs. 27 at 2- 0 p.m.
Thurs. 30 at 2- 0 p.m.	

DOUGLAS TO DUBLIN

MAY.		JUNE.	
Sun. 5 at 4- 0 a.m.	Sat. 1 at midnight
Wed. 8 at 6- 0 a.m.	Wed. 5 at 5- 0 a.m.
Sat. 11 at 9- 0 p.m.	Sat. 8 at 7- 0 p.m.
Wed. 15 at 10- 0 a.m.	Wed. 12 at 9- 0 a.m.
Sun. 19 at 4- 0 a.m.	Sat. 15 at midnight
Wed. 22 at 6- 0 a.m.	Wed. 19 at 5- 0 a.m.
Sat. 25 at 8- 0 p.m.	Sat. 22 at 7- 0 p.m.
Wed. 29 at 10- 0 a.m.	Wed. 26 at 9-30 a.m.
	Sat. 29 at 10-30 p.m.

DOUGLAS TO SILLOTH

Note.—In case of early morning arrivals at Silloth, passengers may remain aboard till 8 a.m.

MAY.		JUNE.	
Thurs. 2 at midnight	Tues. 4 at 3-30 a.m.
Tues. 7 at 3 30 a.m.	Fri. 7 at 5-30 a.m.
Fri. 10 at 6- 0 a.m.	Tues. 11 at 8- 0 a.m.
Tues. 14 at 7- 0 a.m.	Thurs. 13 at 11- 0 a.m.
Fri. 17 at 1- 0 a.m.	Tues. 18 at 3-30 a.m.
Tues. 21 at 4-30 a.m.	Fri. 21 at 5-30 a.m.
Fri. 24 at 5-30 a.m.	Tues. 25 at 7-30 a.m.
Tues. 28 at 7-30 a.m.	Thurs. 27 at 10- 0 a.m.
Thurs. 30 at 11- 0 p.m.	

SILLOTH TO DOUGLAS

Saturday sailing for landing at Douglas, only passengers, and packages not over 1 cwt. accepted.

MAY.		JUNE.	
Sat. 4 at 9- 0 p.m.	Sat. 1 at 6- 0 p.m.
Tues. 7 at 11- 0 p.m.	Tues. 4 at 9-40 p.m.
Sat. 11 at 1-30 p.m.	Sat. 8 at noon
Tues. 14 at *midnight	Tues. 11 at *midnight
Sat. 18 at 9- 0 p.m.	Sat. 15 at 7-30 p.m.
Tues. 21 at 11- 0 p.m.	Tues. 18 at 10- 0 p.m.
Sat. 25 at *1- 0 p.m.	Sat. 22 at noon
Tues. 28 at *midnight	Tues. 25 at *midnight
	Sat. 29 at 4-30 p.m.

*Note :—Steamer sails as soon as tide permits

PASSENGER FARES.

	SINGLE		RETURN	
	Saloon	Steerage	Saloon	Steerage
Between DOUGLAS, I.O.M. and SILLOTH or DUBLIN	12 6	8 0	17 6	12 6
Between DUBLIN and SILLOTH	20 0	12 6	30 0	20 0

For further information apply to—

JOHN METCALFE, Agent,
49 NORTH QUAY, DOUGLAS.

Telegrams : "Metcalfe, Douglas (Man)."   Telephone : Douglas 100.

OR TO

PALGRAVE MURPHY LTD. (Managers)
Head Office: 17 EDEN QUAY, DUBLIN.

Dock Office for Reception of Goods : CUSTOM HOUSE QUAY, NORTH WALL.

Telegrams : "Palgrave, Dublin."   Telephone : Dublin 3576 (3 lines).

The Victoria Press, Martins Bank Chambers, Victoria Street, Douglas.   [SEE OVER]

49

Almost from the outset in 1859, coal had been a major export to Ireland from Silloth Docks. From the several mines in west Cumberland and supplemented by coal from other areas, it was delivered by rail to Silloth. Much of it was then loaded into ships by a hydraulic hoist that lifted the coal wagons and tipped them allowing the coal to flow down a chute and into the ship's holds. This trade continued right up to 1958 and the coal wagon hoist was finally dismantled in 1961.

The hydraulic coal wagon hoist in New Dock, August 1934.

*Captain George Ramsey,
Silloth Dockmaster,
1930-1937.*

Assaroe*, ex **Yarrow**, stopped in New Dock entrance and discharging passengers from Dublin, 1935.*

Records and especially photographs of activities at the port of Silloth during the 2nd World War are proving very hard to find, but anecdotal information would indicate that the port continued to be very busy with exports of coal continuing to Ireland. Silloth was apparently graded as a "safe port" by the wartime Government. Reportedly, large quantities of cased and drummed petroleum products were sent from here to the various military campaigns in North Africa and other locations in the Mediterranean. With these activities and those of the nearby RAF airfield, the whole of the Silloth area was of military significance and therefore access was carefully controlled, with armed checkpoints on all the approach roads.

It is reported that in April 1941, despite flying the Irish tricolour, (being Irish registered), and displaying wartime neutrality markings, the **Assaroe** was attacked and strafed in the Irish Sea by a German aircraft. No serious damage was sustained. She maintained her Silloth – Dublin service until sold in 1943.

A rare 1941 wartime photograph of the New Dock, drained for some reason
and with the dock gates partially opened. A ship lies alongside Carr's flour mill.

RAF air-sea rescue launches occasionally berthed at Silloth pier, on which there was a small cabin, occupied by the launch crews. Reportedly, during 1942, an oil lamp in that cabin caused a fire, which resulted in the loss of the extreme end of the pier.

Silloth's Docks immediately after the Second World War.

At the end of the Second World War there was a huge surplus of bombs and other munitions, which had to be disposed of. Dumping at sea was the accepted method and one of the few allocated disposal areas was the Beaufort Dyke, a deep trench in the North Channel between Northern Ireland and the Mull of Galloway. Silloth was selected as a suitable port from which to transport these munitions to the dumping ground.

RASC bomb dumping escort vessels in New Dock, c.1947-1949.

Tank landing craft were initially used as the means of transporting unwanted munitions out to the dumping ground, until one was sunk in bad weather off Burrow Head, with the loss of her crew in January 1946. After that, the Royal Army Service Corps commandeered small coastal traders for the task. The dumping process then continued right up until May 1949 without further serious incident.

*Bomb dumping from the RASC vessel **Marquis of Hartington**, c.1947-1949.*
She was a commissioned vessel manned by a civilian crew.

In 1948, the veteran paddle tug **Petrel** was finally taken out of service and laid up for scrap.

*Paddle tug **Petrel** seen here in the Marshall Dock.*

In 1948, the British railway system was nationalised. Ownership of Silloth Docks, which had always belonged to one railway company or another, was transferred to The Docks and Inland Waterways Executive, as part of the state-owned British Transport Commission.

The truncated Silloth pier, as a result of an accidental fire during 1942.
*The vessel in the foreground is the **Gypsy Queen**.*

1950 – 1979

During the 1950s trade consisted mainly of imports of grain for Carr's mill, potash and phosphates for the fertiliser industry, perlite and slag for the building industry, with occasional cargoes of sugar and steel billets (ingot moulds). Exports were coal to Ireland, fertilisers and bran.

*The J. S. Monks coaster **Bankville** discharging grain from Liverpool,*
c.1950.

c. early 1950s. Silloth channel buoys being maintained in the New Dock. On the buoy, note the dog named "Chance" belonging to dock worker Stan Greenway, which he had rescued from the waters of the Canada Dock, Liverpool!

Early 1950s view of Silloth station and the network of rail tracks leading to the docks and flour mill in the background. The long structure on the left is the cargo transit shed sited on the south side of the New Dock.

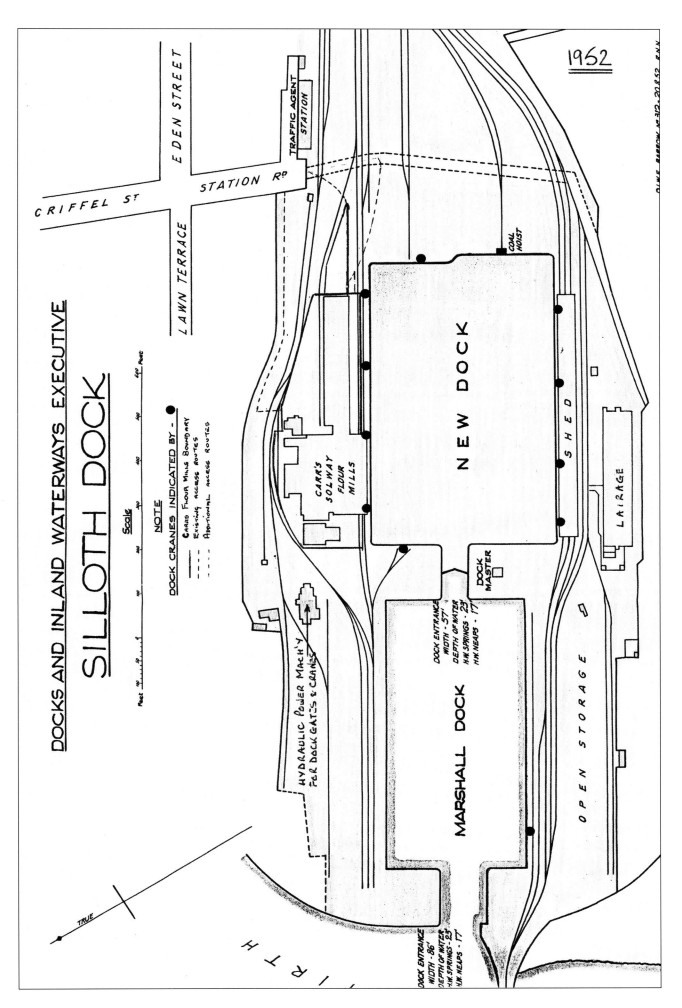

DOCKS AND INLAND WATERWAYS EXECUTIVE

SILLOTH DOCK

1952

NEW DOCK

MARSHALL DOCK

CARR'S SOLWAY FLOUR MILLS

SHED

LAIRAGE

OPEN STORAGE

HYDRAULIC POWER MACH'Y FOR DOCK GATES & CRANES

DOCK MASTER

COAL HOIST

TRAFFIC AGENT STATION

EDEN STREET

CRIFFEL ST

STATION RD

LAWN TERRACE

DOCK ENTRANCE
WIDTH - 57'
DEPTH OF WATER
H.W. SPRINGS - 23'
H.W. NEAPS - 17'

DOCK ENTRANCE
WIDTH - 86'
DEPTH OF WATER
H.W. SPRINGS - 23'
H.W. NEAPS - 17'

FIRTH

TRUE

Scale

Feet

NOTE

DOCK CRANES INDICATED BY -

● CARR'S FLOUR MILLS BOUNDARY

——— EXISTING ACCESS ROUTES

- - - - ADDITIONAL ACCESS ROUTES

57

Tragedy Strikes

On Monday 10 December 1956 at about 4.30pm, Silloth Fire Brigade, manned by volunteer firemen, answered a distress signal, which stated that a wildfowler was believed to be in difficulties in Moricambe Bay, the bay being a wide, shallow estuary for the rivers Waver and Wampool. The bay is located about four miles north of the town and is a popular feeding ground for geese, ducks and a wide variety of wading birds.

With no lifeboat stationed in the area at that time, the Fire Station at Silloth was equipped with a light aluminium rescue craft and outboard motor for such emergencies and this was taken by trailer to Grune Point, on the southern entrance to the bay. It was launched with four men on board, Stanley Graham (29), Joseph Bell (37), coxswain Alex Ramsay (45), and a recent recruit and eldest of the four, Silloth dock worker John (Jockey) Johnstone (47).

Darkness was falling and with a steadily increasing wind strength, the seas were high with a fast running ebb tide. As the men set off into the bay they were soon swallowed up by the darkness. The weather grew steadily worse through the evening, until about midnight, after which the skies gradually cleared and the weather moderated.

But at 7.30 pm that evening and with no sight or sign from the boat, there were growing concerns for the men's safety. Workington lifeboat, located some twenty miles south of Silloth, was called out whilst a fire tender at the point the boat was launched scoured the water with its searchlight. Lights were kept on at the nearby air stations of Anthorn, Kirkbride and Silloth, in the hope that they would be a useful guide for the boat's crew. Coastguards and police patrolled the edges of the bay in case the men had come ashore in an isolated location. An appeal for helicopter assistance was turned down, it being unable to operate at night.

As dawn broke the following morning, the worst fears were realised when the boat was found, with no survivors. It was discovered by Workington lifeboat, aground on a sandbank out in the bay, following which the lifeboat itself became stuck aground for several hours. A daylight search by aircraft located three of the bodies, whilst the fourth was not recovered until more than a week later on the Scottish coast.

It was thought that the boat had become overwhelmed by the choppy sea, or had struck a sandbank, throwing the men overboard. Nothing more was heard of the unknown person that the four local firemen had bravely set out to rescue.

Thirty years later a local newspaper recalled the tragedy in the article reproduced on the following page.

An SOS call . . . and four brave men died

Tragic heroes of the cruel sea...

JOHN JOHNSTONE

STANLEY GRAHAM

JOSEPH BELL

ALEX RAMSAY

THE drama began at four o'clock in the afternoon of December 10.

Wildfowler Robert Robinson, who was shooting on Skinburness marsh, saw a man struggling.

The man was a mile away but Mr Robinson, using his binoculars, saw that he was up to his shoulders in water.

He ran two miles to the nearest phone to raise the alarm.

Storm

Police Sergeant Chris Hodgson received the message at Silloth and alerted the docks at Silloth and the Royal Naval Air Station at Anthorn.

Anthorn said that it would take two hours to prepare a helicopter and by then it would be too dark for it to operate.

By this time the local part-time fire brigade, which also operated the sea rescue boat at that time, was swinging into action.

The weather was fine although there was a strong wind and rough seas.

Unfortunately the strong wind brought heavy rain and there was a storm until 10.30 p.m., a factor which was to have a tragic bearing on the night's events.

George Falder drove the fire service vehicle with the 14-foot aluminium boat and three of the four crew to near Grune Point, where it was to be launched.

The fourth member of the crew, John Johnstone, arrived soon afterwards on the pillion of a motor-cycle.

Mr Falder advised the men not to go out to the sea as it was running high but one of them said that they would just go across to an area known as the Target and look for the man there.

Fears

The four men used their oars until they were in deeper water, when they started their outboard motor.

Mr Falder said he could see only about 100 yards without the use of his vehicle lights.

Then the tiny boat disappeared into the darkness of the storm.

By 7.30 p.m. there were fears for the safety of the men and a huge search operation involving 100 men was mounted.

Workington lifeboat found the capsized rescue boat and was then itself involved in high drama.

The lifeboat grounded on a sand bank for eighteen hours and food was dropped to the crew.

Winter

Constant signalling was kept up through the night by a searchlight from one of the fire tenders at Grune Point.

In the forlorn hope of providing beacons for the missing firemen, all lights blazed at the Silloth and Anthorn airfields.

Police cars patrolled the coast road to help any survivors.

Two Silloth fishing boats helped in the search but had to give up because of the darkness.

When it became light four planes and a helicopter from Anthorn joined the hunt.

EXACTLY thirty years ago this week four part-time Silloth firemen drowned while searching for a wildfowler believed to be in difficulties on a marsh.

The small town where the men lived was stunned by the tragedy.

DAVID HAY re-tells the story of the cockleshell heroes.

It wasn't until that morning that two of the bodies were washed up, one at Silloth, the other at Skinburness.

Shore

A third body was discovered later that morning at Skinburness and the fourth body was found on the shore on the Scottish side of the Solway.

As no other body was ever found and no wildfowler ever came forward to say he had been in difficulty on the marsh that night, many people felt that the four men had given their lives for nothing.

But the inquest coroner and jury were assured by witnesses that there had been a fifth man on the marsh.

Waves

The only clue to the men's fate came from the county chief fire officer, Mr J. McIntyre.

He told the coroner that he was convinced that the boat would not sink and would have ridden the high waves.

He felt that the boat must have struck the bottom in shallow water and been thrown over by a wave, giving the men no chance to grab the ropes.

THE oldest of the four heroes was John Johnstone, a 47-year-old dock worker.

He had been a volunteer fireman for only a few weeks and the rescue attempt was the first one in which he had taken part.

Mr Johnstone left a widow and three daughters, aged 22, 19 and 18.

He had held a number of offices in Silloth Methodist Chapel, was a keen golfer, and a former Cumberland and Westmorland Rugby Union player.

The youngest member of the crew was Stanley Graham, 29, a joiner. He left a widow and two girls, aged 5 and 8.

Joseph Bell, a 37-year-old school caretaker, played rugby for Silloth. He left a widow and two children, aged 7 and 8.

Alex Ramsay, a 45-year-old motor engineer, left a widow and a son of nine.

'They went with no thought for themselves'

The Rev. J. E. Bebb, Vicar of Silloth, said of the four men: "They were four of the finest fellows in Silloth. They went out with no thought for themselves."

Night of tragedy

PRESSMEN from virtually every national newspaper travelled to Silloth to record the events of that terrible night.

Local journalist Dick Allen and Cumberland News chief photographer Peter Dunn were first on the scene.

Dick recalls: "We were taken out to Grune Point by fire tender.

"It was pitch black, pouring with rain, and the waves were 20ft. high.

"We felt even then that there could be little hope for anyone missing in such atrocious conditions.

"It was a night that none us will ever forget.

"The late Wilson Little, manager of the Skinburness Hotel, opened up the building which was closed for the winter, and it was used as a rest and refreshment centre for the nurses, WVS ladies, police and firemen.

"Wilson even lit fires to warm the rescue parties."

Nation's thanks

HAROLD MACMILLAN
Sent letter

THE coroner at the inquest, Col. F. W. Halton, said he would recommend the four men for posthumous awards.

Both the Queen and the then Prime Minister, Harold MacMillan, responded.

The bereaved families received a letter of condolence from MacMillan and the Queen sent the widows a brooch commemorating the bravery of their husbands.

59

January 1958.
Discharging steel billets from the m.v. **Pegasus**, *for Distington Engineering Works Ltd at Workington. The* **Cairngorm** *behind, is loading the final consignment of coal from Silloth Docks, bound for Dublin.*

March 1959. Yet another section of the pier collapses .....

.... and eventually disappears.

23 June 1960.
Manchester Venture *discharges wheat from Port Arthur, Canada.*

In 1963, the ownership of the port of Silloth changed when the British Transport Commission was dissolved. The new owners were the British Transport Docks Board.

January 1964.
Carr's flour and animal feed mills.
In the background the coaster **Pioneer** *is discharging grain from Amsterdam*

An aerial view of Silloth and the docks, July 1961.

As the result of a cost saving report in 1963 by the Chairman of British Rail, Dr Beeching, many rural or little used branch rail lines were to be progressively closed as being uneconomic. Consequently, 6 September 1964 saw the final closure of the railway line from Carlisle to Silloth, thus ending over 100 years of that important commercial transport link to the town and the port. Although apparently closed as unprofitable at the time, it was a facility that is much missed by the townspeople to this present day. Had it survived, the tourism potential of that scenic railway route could possibly have been exploited to enhance greatly the fortunes of the still attractive Victorian seaside town of Silloth.

*Prior to closure, a special train at Silloth on 13 June 1964, with two preserved locomotives. A Caley Single No.123 is connected to the carriages and in front, the GNSR **Gordon Highlander** No.49.*

Between 1965 and 1967 the Ardmore Steel Company set up a ship-breaking business on the south side of the Marshall Dock, cutting up nine ships in all during that period, including two former Royal Navy minesweepers, the **Niger** and the **Chameleon**.

*HMS **Chameleon** (M387) and HMS **Niger** (M73) and the **S.E.Cooper** in various stages of being broken up in Marshall Dock.*

30 April 1966.
*The **Firth Fisher** in the New Dock, having arrived from Manchester with a large cylinder for Thames Board Mills at Workington. A railway bridge at that time prevented access to the mill for large loads arriving through the port of Workington.*

1967 - Silloth Lifeboat Station Re-Established

Possibly as a result of the tragic loss of the four Silloth firemen back in 1956, or as a result of local public pressure, or following a routine coastal reassessment by RNLI Inspectors, Silloth Lifeboat Station was re-opened on 1 August 1967. Manned as always by local volunteers, the station was equipped with a small inshore, inflatable "D" class lifeboat, (D-146), using the same Victorian boathouse that had housed the earlier wooden lifeboats. The first crewmen for the lifeboat were Alan Ray and Bill Irving, both local fishermen, Ivan Lomas, a Silloth fishmonger, George Egdell, a school teacher, and Colin Akitt, a Silloth dockworker.

The Silloth "D" class lifeboat (D-144).

The D-146 was replaced by D-144 in 1969, which remained the station lifeboat until 4 June 1975. She was then replaced by a trial Mk5 Zodiac (D-502), called **John Gilpin**, which in turn was replaced by a similar craft, the D-503 in September 1977. This boat design was eventually considered unsuitable for RNLI purposes and taken out of service, but not before a split transom on the Silloth lifeboat caused problems and quick remedial thinking by the crew, while out on a rescue service in the Solway.

*15 June 1975. Launching the **John Gilpin** (D-502).*
(Cumberland Newspapers Group Limited)

On 6 June 1979, Silloth Lifeboat Station took delivery of its first Atlantic 21 class of inshore lifeboat, **Major Osman Gabriel** (B-505), for suitability trials on the Solway Firth. These boats were much larger and faster than the "D" class boats and of a rigid-inflatable design, having inflatable sponsons mounted on a rigid glass fibre keel and deck section. By 1980 the trials had proved successful and Silloth received its own Atlantic 21 class, the **Amelia Gregory Armstrong** (B-545). That year, the lifeboat house was modified to accommodate a tractor, capable of hauling the boat and its launching trailer up and down the precariously steep slipway or to alternative launch sites.

*Silloth lifeboat **Amelia Gregory Armstrong** (1980 – 1995)*
and the Victorian lifeboat house.

In 1992, plans were laid to replace the ageing **Amelia** with one of the next generation of inshore lifeboats, which were still undergoing design trials. The old Victorian boathouse would no longer be large enough to accept the new lifeboat and its equipment and the steep slipway would have to be replaced. Work on both these projects began in 1994 and the lifeboat moved to temporary accommodation at Silloth Docks. In April that year an Appeal was launched locally, to raise £61,000 to cover the cost of the new Silloth lifeboat, which would be of the Atlantic 75 class.

Completed in March of 1995, a splendid newly built boathouse now stands proudly on the site of the previous building. Its structure neatly incorporates some of the original stonework and roof slates from the earlier Victorian building. By April that year, the new and longer slipway was completed and **Amelia** happily returned to her new home. By the end of June, the Appeal had reached its target and on 27 June 1995, the new Atlantic 75 class, **Spirit of Cumbria** (B714), arrived on station. The lifeboat was officially named by HRH The Duchess of Kent on 11 October that same year.

Silloth lifeboat **Spirit of Cumbria** *(1995 - 2008).*

The **Spirit of Cumbria** proved very successful during her tenure as the Silloth Lifeboat, carrying out numerous rescues and other services in the upper Solway area. The RNLI have a policy of providing the best possible equipment for their volunteer crews and to that end and having served on the front line for 13 years, the **Spirit of Cumbria** was transferred to the RNLI reserve fleet. She has been replaced at Silloth by the very latest in inshore lifeboat design, one of the new Atlantic 85 class, **Elaine and Don Wilkinson** (B-828), named after her benefactors. She took over station duties in November 2008 and is due to be officially named later in 2009.

Silloth lifeboat **Elaine and Don Wilkinson** *(2008 – date).*

Silloth Docks (1950 – 1979)

The old and leaking timber dock gates at the entrance to New Dock, which had been fitted when the dock was built in 1885, were replaced in 1967 by a new pair of steel gates. Built in the shipyard at Barrow in Furness, they were laid on their side and towed to Silloth. Once here, they were ballasted to float upright at the correct depth then floated into position and secured. As with the wooden pair, the new gates were to be drawn open and closed by steel chains connected to quayside winches. This system was superceded in 1990, when the chains were replaced by powerful hydraulic rams.

8 May 1967.
*The Mersey-based tug **Trafalgar**, arriving in the New Dock*
with one of a pair of new steel fabricated dock gates.

1968 was the year when a new animal lairage was built on the south side of New Dock, which could accommodate up to 600 head of cattle. Since the 1880s, Irish cattle had been imported through Silloth, both on the **Yarrow** and later on ships specially adapted for the carriage of livestock. The dilapidated remains of a long quayside transit shed and the remaining parts of an earlier cattle lairage built in 1913, had to be cleared to make room for this large prefabricated structure. In 1978 a second smaller lairage building was added and cattle continued to be imported up until 1989. Nowadays, Irish beef is shipped over in freezer lorries via Stranraer or other ferry ports.

Opening day of the new lairage building, 26 July 1968.

December 1977.
The cattle being discharged
*from the **Frisian Express**.*

*The **Frisian Express**
sails back to Ireland.*

An overhead view of the town and docks in August 1968.
All railway tracks removed and note the remaining pier stump.

In the early hours of Sunday 20 June 1971, a serious fire swept through Carr's flour mill, gutting the top two floors, causing some serious damage to other parts of the building and to flour stocks. From the ashes of that setback, there quickly grew a modern and efficient milling facility, which continues to produce top quality blends of flour for today's discerning bakers.

Serious fire at Carr's flour mill, 20 June 1971.
(Cumberland News)

During 1973, the last remaining portion of the once magnificent Silloth pier was finally demolished. Completed in 1857 and originally 1000 feet long, it was built on timber piles driven into the hard clay below the beach. It afforded some protection to the harbour entrance, a rather exposed berth for small shipping at all stages of the tide and a magnificent view up and down the Solway Firth. Sections of it had gradually subsided and collapsed since the 1920s, probably due to the foundation piles being undermined by the scouring of a shifting channel and the work of marine boring worms. It was replaced by a short timber groyne to prevent beach material blocking the dock entrance, and marked by three timber dolphins.

Dismantling the remains of Silloth pier, 1973.

28 February 1975.
Marshall Dock entrance, with the new timber groyne on the south side
and marked by three timber dolphins.

In 1974, a small shipping company was established at Silloth, eventually operating three vessels, the **Silloth Pride**, the **Silloth Trader** and the **Silloth Stag**. The vessels traded between European ports and the UK, including carrying wheat cargoes from Liverpool to Silloth. Unfortunately, trading conditions became increasingly difficult and the company eventually folded in 1981.

*1974. The Master and crew of the **Silloth Trader** at Silloth Docks.*

On 21 August 1976, HMS **Crichton**, a timber-built Ton-class minesweeper in New Dock made an overnight call to Silloth. She had arrived the previous evening and was commanded by Lt Cdr Richard Williams RNR, who was born locally at Aspatria and educated at Nelson Tomlinson School in nearby Wigton. Manned by a Royal Naval Reserve crew, the warship was taking a brief respite from a weekend exercise in the Irish Sea. Unfortunately, and much to the disappointment of local people who came to the dock to see the vessel, she was not opened to the public during her brief visit. A warship visit to the port of Silloth is an extremely rare occurrence. There are no records of any previous warship visit, nor any to date since the **Crichton**, other than annual calls since 2005 by Silloth's associated university training patrol boat HMS **Biter**.

22 August 1976.

The timber-built Ton-class minesweeper about to depart from Silloth's New Dock following her overnight stay.
(the late Frank Wright, courtesy Stephen Wright)

12 June 1977.
*The **Albert-S** discharging ground nuts (animal feed) from Dakar,*
*whilst astern the **Therese** discharges pumice from the Lipari Islands.*

*March 1978.
Silloth's shrimping fleet,
moored in Marshall Dock.*

*The two photographs above
can be contrasted with
these alongside and below
which depict the shrimping
vessels of the 1920s.*

On 29 July 1980, the widest recorded vessel to enter the New Dock, the **Aberthaw Fisher** (beam 16,5 metres), arrived to discharge a 103 ton machine glazing cylinder for Thames Board Mills, (now Iggesund), at Workington. The dock entrance is 18 metres wide at the top and just 16,15 metres at the bottom. Careful planning was necessary to ensure the tide was high enough for the bilges of the ship to pass through the entrance. All quayside fendering had to be temporarily removed.

July 1980.
*The **Aberthaw Fisher** squeezes out having discharged her load.*

In 1982, Blue Circle started to export large quantities of cement powder from their factory at Stanhope in Weardale, via Silloth Docks, to Magheramorne, in Northern Ireland. Cement was initially blown into the ship's hold directly from lorries, until the port's stevedore D A Harrison constructed a special storage facility on the dockside which could be filled as necessary and then gravity fed into ships when they arrived.

Assembly of three cement powder silos at the eastern end of New Dock, 1983.

31 May 1984
After arrival from Stornoway, the **Ligar Bay** loads cement for Ramsey whilst a Blue Circle
lorry simultaneously discharges into the silos.
(Dr Brunhead collection)

9 April 1983.
The Dutch coaster **Mercurius** awaits departure. She had been built in 1959
as a conventional coaster but in 1974 was converted to carry cement
after the fitting of six spherical tanks in her hold.
(Bernard McCall)

10 December 1983.
The **Mercurius** sails with the Solway navigation buoy in tow and the buoy sinker lashed alongside.
She later dropped the sinker and cut the buoy free in a designated position at the entrance to the
Silloth approaches. She was a regular caller, loading for Northern Ireland and the Isle of Man
between 1982 and 1988 whenshe caught fire and was abandoned off the Hebrides.
She had been bought by Blue Circle and renamed **B C Mercurius** in 1987.

13 June 1983.
The **Activity** arriving with 1254 tonnes of molasses from Liverpool, to be discharged into a small
storage tank on the dock, for Carr's Agriculture Division. In the foreground is the remains of a wooden
cofferdam, which filled a gap in the dock wall, left open for possible future expansion of the dock
system if trade demanded. It was never required and the wall was later sealed with steel sheet piling.
In the background, the **Udo** discharges 1316 tonnes of grain from Delfzijl.

During 1983, the British Transport Docks Board was privatised, now becoming Associated British Ports PLC. All the 21 ports within the group, which included widely diverse activities such as those at Southampton, Hull, Swansea and Silloth, were now the joint property of very demanding shareholders.

A 1983 aerial view of Silloth Docks and the town, looking north-eastwards towards Grune Point and Moricambe Bay (not to be confused with Morecambe Bay in Lancashire!). Top right in the photo can be seen part of the old RAF wartime airfield. Built in 1938, it was used extensively for the training of aircrew for Coastal Command, as well as the servicing and maintenance of a wide variety of military aircraft, including Hudson and Wellington bombers. The airfield finally closed when the RAF moved out in 1960.

(Airviews [M/cr] Ltd)

April 1987.
*A rare accident, when the **Edgar Dorman** lost steering,and struck*
the entrance knuckle of the New Dock.

November 1988.
***Gerhard Prahm** loading an awkward 24 tonne piece of machinery for a factory at Bideford.*

Throughout the 1980s and early 1990s, milk powder was exported from the Nestle factory at Dalston near Carlisle, to Jeddah in Saudi Arabia, as well as to the central American countries and the West Indies.

September 1987.
*The **Tequila Sunrise** loading milk powder for El Salvador.*

September 1993
*The **Baltic Trader** arrives from Port Harcourt, West Africa, with animal feed for*
*Carr's Agricultural Division, whilst the **Gorch Fock** discharges French wheat to Carr's flour mill.*

At 114 metres, the longest recorded vessel to arrive at Silloth, the **Sovietskiy Sever** arrived from St Petersburg on 17 January 1995 with a cargo of fertiliser. The New Dock is only 120m wide, allowing very little room to turn the ship. Fortunately there were no other vessels in dock at that time, allowing her to swing and berth alongside.

January 1995.
*The **Sovietskiy Sever** swinging in the New Dock.*

During 1995 and 1996, two shipments of Chilean alpacas were quarantined within the lairage at Silloth Docks. Valued for their woolly fleece, which can be sheared in a similar fashion to that of sheep, they were brought to this country for the purpose of establishing a breeding stock. Originally flown from Chile into Manchester airport, each shipment consisted of 300 adult animals. They were then brought to Silloth Docks by road transport, to remain in quarantine for approximately four months. Some of the female adults turned out to be pregnant and produced beautiful calves. The animals were cared for by Mr Wallace Bisset, who had previously been manager of the modern lairage during the latter days of cattle imports.

Alpacas in Silloth Dock lairage, 1996.

Refurbishment of the East Cote lighthouse in 1997. Located on the foreshore to the north of the dock and originally built as a leading light in transit with the Lees Scar lighthouse and later with a light on the end of Silloth pier, it now shines a steady beam of green light down the Silloth approach channel.

The Silloth Team, March 2000. Back Row: Colin Akitt (Leading Dockgateman), Capt. Bill Amyes (Pilot), Ken Winter, (Dockgateman). Front Row: Alan Ray (Pilot), Capt. Chris Puxley (Harbour Master), David Gardiner (Pilot).

Taking mutiny too far!
*A visit by the theatre ship **Fitzcarraldo** in August 1996*
instigates a minor uprising by local children
against the Harbour Master Capt. Chris Puxley.

(Cumberland News)

July 2001
*A pilot's eye view as the **Louise Trader** arrives at Silloth from Spain with a cargo of*
wood pulp for the UCB Films (now Innovia Films Ltd) factory at Wigton.

Ships bound for Silloth are boarded by an experienced pilot at the pilot station located about a mile and a half off the port of Workington. The pilot then navigates the ship for the final fifteen miles through the difficult shifting channels of the upper Solway Firth and into the port of Silloth. Ordinary mariners are warned on charts and in Admiralty publications that they should not attempt to navigate these waters without local knowledge.

15 August 2001.
*The **Crescent Seine** continues discharging wheat to Carr's mill whilst*
sitting on the mud during repairs to the dock gates.

Dredging of the New Dock is a function that needs to be carried out every three or four years, depending on the rate of siltation. The very slow but gradual increase of the mud level within the New Dock is caused every time the dock gates are opened, thus allowing the natural sediment of the Solway Firth, which is held in suspension, to come in with the rising tide. Within the still waters of the dock, the sediment settles to the bottom. Whenever possible, the dock gates are kept shut to prevent the build up of silt, but they have to be opened near high water for shipping movements and whenever the following tide is of greater height than its predecessor, i.e. when progressing from neap tides to spring tides.

The channel through the outer Marshall Dock and the outer dock entrance is kept clear of silt and beach material by opening sluice paddles at low water. These sluices are located in the dock wall, either side of the New Dock entrance. This allows a controlled rush of water to flow out of the New Dock and wash out the Marshall Dock channel and port entrance.

July 2000.
*The grab dredger **Cherry Sand** working in the New Dock.*
She is the only dredger of her type in the fleet of UK Dredging,
a subsidiary company of Associated British Ports.
When fully loaded she will exit the dock near high water and release her load
through bottom doors at an approved dump site or spoil ground in the Solway Firth.

26 June 2002.
*The crowds come to welcome the sailing vessel **Phoenix** to Silloth. **Phoenix** has*
appeared in various guises and in several period films, including the TV series of 'Hornblower'.
The port office is in the background.

February 2003.
*The **Heljo**, discharging 3311 tonnes of fertiliser, a record cargo for Silloth at that time.*

During 2002, a major export commodity ceased with the closure of the cement factory in Weardale. Fortunately however, a new opportunity arose with the building of a liquid molasses terminal for Prime Molasses and the subsequent importing of that product in tankers for the animal feed business.

6 August 2004.
*The tanker **British Shield** turns in New Dock prior to discharging*
nearly 3000 tonnes of molasses from Le Havre.
(Stephen Wright)

In 2005 the Royal Navy vessel HMS **Biter** was affiliated with the town of Silloth. HMS **Biter** is a fast patrol craft of the **Archer** class and allocated to the Manchester and Salford Universities' Royal Navy Unit. Her main role is the training of undergraduates who have expressed an interest in the Royal Navy. Whilst with the RN Unit they are classed as Midshipmen (and women). She usually tries to visit Silloth for a weekend every March/April.

March 2005.
*HMS **Biter** attracts an interested crowd of onlookers.*

Another attraction at the port during the summers of 2005, 2006 and 2007 has been the replica man-of-war **Grand Turk**. Faithfully built on the lines of the 18th century warship HMS **Blandford** she made a fine sight for locals and visitors to step aboard and explore.

The **Grand Turk** entering New Dock 2007.

Cargo tonnage records have continued to rise over recent years. At the time of writing, the largest tonnage handled at Silloth stands at 4152 tonnes, which was a cargo discharged for Carr's fertilisers from the **Arklow River** in March 2008. In addition to large volumes of imported fertilisers, the port continues to handle considerable quantities of imported and home grown wheat, plus liquid molasses and baled wood pulp for local industries.

March 2008.
*The **Arklow Rive**r, having discharged over 4000 tonnes of*
fertiliser from Beverwijk in Holland, manoeuvres to sail to her next destination.

A small resident fishing fleet, moored in the Marshall Dock, continues to trawl the Solway channels for the delicious brown shrimps which are boiled aboard the boats before landing and exported, as well as going on sale in the town, fresh or potted as required. Licences are occasionally granted by the Cumbria Sea Fisheries Committee for the gathering of cockles and mussels from the Solway beds.

*One of the current Silloth shrimp boats **Jolanda**,*
built at Silloth in 1990 and owned by the Ray family.

7 April 2008.
*The **Victress** arriving with 2245 tonnes of fertiliser from IJmuiden.*
(Stephen Wright)

8 April 2008.
*The **Potosi**, sailing to Glasgow in ballast, having discharged 3348 tonnes of fertiliser from Sfax, Tunisia.*
(Stephen Wright)

1 May 2008.
*The **Seawheel Express** discharged 2511 tonnes of bagged fertiliser from Batumi, Georgia.*
(Stephen Wright)

3 May 2008.

*Having discharged her cargo, the **Seawheel Express** leaves Silloth at the start of a voyage to Rotterdam.*
(Stephen Wright)

Although a multi-purpose ship, she was designed mainly for work in the container trades and her name revealed that she had been on charter to the Seawheel company for its container feeder services. In this view she is heading down the Solway Firth (Derek McAlone)

October 2008.

*The Norwegian live fish carrier **Gripfisk** loading live salmon smolt.*

The fish are bred at Armathwaite and Haweswater in Cumbria, then transported by lorry to the dock in freshwater tanks, where they are then piped into large seawater tanks on board the vessel for carriage to fish farms around Scotland.

(A smolt is a young salmon, which is just old enough to cope with the transition from fresh to seawater – as it would quite naturally when swimming from river breeding grounds to spend its adult life in the sea).

The port of Silloth takes its environmental responsibilities seriously and as a result a wide variety of wild life abound on the port estate, a large part of which is designated a site of Special Scientific Interest, mainly due to the local coastal dune system and the presence of colonies of the rare great crested newt and the natterjack toad. The port is also surrounded by the Solway Coast Area of Outstanding Natural Beauty. In addition to the regular views of birds such as stonechats, redshanks, curlews, oystercatchers, turnstones, dunlins, cormorants, swans, herons, guillemots, greylag and barnacle geese and a wide variety of gulls, there have been recent sightings of kingfishers, a great northern diver, a red-necked grebe, gooseanders and the annual winter arrival of small diving ducks such as the scaup. Animals include of course the prolific rabbits, as well as a resident stoat, the occasional and inquisitive grey seal and currently an otter.

18 October 2008.
The Dutch tugs **Andre-B** and **Multratug 17**, sheltering from autumnal gales. Both tugs are employed in the construction of a 60 turbine offshore windfarm at Robin Rigg in the Solway Firth.

27 October 2008.
The Cyprus-registered tanker **Wigry**, discharging 3130 tonnes of molasses.

The Future?

The Port of Silloth, under the ownership and management of Associated British Ports, looks confidently towards the future. The docks continue to play an integral role in the Cumbrian and regional economy and are a catalyst for local trade and commerce. Whilst maintaining a steady customer base, mainly thanks to the successful flour milling and agricultural divisions of 'Carr's Milling Industries', the port is always looking to expand that base and to diversify into other commodities.

Here at the Port of Silloth we are fortunate to have a very flexible and willing workforce in our licensed stevedoring company 'D.A.Harrison', which is an essential factor for smaller ports, if they are to be able to compete for business in tough economic times.

The recent worldwide fluctuations in fuel costs, coupled with tough economic and environmental pressures, may soon favourably affect the prospects for the increased use of short sea transportation of goods. This would ease pressure on our overcrowded road networks, possibly resulting in an upturn in trade and financial security for the numerous smaller ports dotted around our coastline.

As you will have seen through the pages of this book, the first 150 years in the life of Silloth Docks have thrown up a broad mixture of challenges. The fact that the port is still here, still very much operational, and providing a reliable and quality services to its customers, is very good news for all concerned. In early June 2009, a ship brought a cargo of grain direct from Canada, the first since the 1960s.

I have every confidence that the port will continue to serve its customers and the community for very many years to come. I therefore hope you will join me in a toast, *"To Silloth Docks and the next 150 years"*.

Chris Puxley,
Harbour Master & Port Superintendent.
The Port of Silloth. (1990 to date)

Sunset and the East Cote Lighthouse.

PORT OF SILLOTH

SHIPPING RECORD BREAKERS TO DATE (MAY 2009)

LARGEST CARGO TONNAGES

1. **Arklow River**. 25 March 2008. **4152** tonnes bulk fertiliser from Beverwijk.
2. **King David** (Barque). 21 August 1895. **3937** tonnes wheat from Geelong, Australia.
3. **Anmi**. 2 April 2007. **3901** tonnes bulk fertiliser from Terneuzen, Netherlands.
4. **Pur-Navolok**. 6 July 2008. **3573** tonnes bulk fertiliser from Sfax, Tunisa.
5. **Wilson Tees**. 10 April 2009. **3500** tonnes bulk fertiliser from Sagunto, Spain.
6. **Irena**. 6 November 1907. **3485** tonnes bagged wheat from Braila, River Danube.
7. **Antari**. 11 April 2006. **3422** tonnes bulk fertiliser from IJmuiden, Netherlands.
8. **Antari**. 20 March 2007. **3385** tonnes bulk fertiliser from Ghent, Belgium.
9. **Potosi**. 6 April 2008. **3348** tonnes bulk fertiliser from Sfax, Tunisa.
10. **Jason**. 7 May 2008. **3347** tonnes bulk fertiliser from Sfax, Tunisa.
11. **Heljo**. 2 February 2003. **3311** tonnes bulk fertiliser from Ellesmere Port, UK.
12. **Celtic Pioneer**. 25 February 2009. **3297** tonnes bulk fertiliser from Sagunto, Spain.
13. **Steyning**. 26 October 1987. **3282** tonnes bulk cement clinker to Magheramorne, NI.
14. **British Shield**. 22 November 2003. **3214** tonnes liquid molasses from Barry, UK.

LONGEST VESSELS
(Width of New Dock, within which the vessel must turn around, is 120m.)

1. **Sovietskiy Sever**. 17 January 1995. **113,9m LOA**. Fertiliser from St Petersburg.
2. **Britannia**. 4 September 1903. **110m LOA**. Part cargo of timber, origin unknown.
3. **Michael E. Tricoglu**. July 1929. **105m LOA**. Phosphates from Sfax.
4. **Ludwig Groedel**. 10 September 1906. **105m LOA**. Wheat/timber from Constanta.
5. **Cairngorm**. 7 August 1908. **105m LOA**. Wheat of unknown origin.
6. **Felix De Abasolo**. 30 September 1908. **105m LOA**. Wheat from Romania.
7. **Aggi**. 8 January 1897. **103m LOA**. Part cargo wheat from San Francisco.
8. **Ambassador**. 14 May 1904. **100m LOA**. Wheat of unknown origin.
9. **Gizella Groedel**. 20 June 1905. **100m LOA**. Wheat/timber from Constanta.
10. **Clan Chisholm**. 24 May 1914. **100m LOA**. Guano from Seychelles.
11. **Schulenburg**. 8 December 2004. **99,8m LOA**. Fertiliser from St Petersburg.
12. **Blairmore**. 11 August 1907. **98m LOA**. Wheat from Galatz, River Danube.
13. **British Shield**. 22 November 2003. **97,9m LOA**. Molasses from Barry.

WIDEST VESSELS
(Width of New Dock entrance is 16,15m at the bottom and 18.0m at the top.)

1. **Aberthaw Fisher**. 29 July 1980. **16,5m beam**. Machinery for Thames Board Mill, Workington. The ship was only able to pass through when the tide height lifted the keel above 2.60m from the entrance bottom.
2. **Tequila Sunrise**. 3 September 1987. **15,5m beam**. Milk powder to South America.
3. **A. Andreev**. 11 January 1959. **14,9m beam**. Basic slag from Archangel.
4. **Zapadnyy**. 8 October 2006. **14,4m beam**. Liquid molasses from Bremen.

Silloth Scenes

A splendid view of the railway station and goods yards with the dock and Carr's mill in the distance.

The pier and "Tommy Legs" viewed from the West Beach.

The paddle tug **Petrel** *passes the pier on her way into port.*
From a postcard written on 27 July 1906.

(Bernard McCall collection)

PORT OF SILLOTH
DOCK / HARBOUR MASTERS

1860	Mr Carruthers
1883	Mr George Mundell
1899 - 1930	Mr George Irving
1930 - 1937	Mr George Ramsey
1937 - 1941	Mr J Anderson
1941 - 1962	Capt. William Patterson
1962 - 1968	Capt. R. J. Nicholls
1968 - 1971	Capt. Stuart Bradley
1971 - 1975	Capt. Campbell
1975 - 1990	Capt. John Myers
1990 - date	Capt. Chris Puxley

This postcard image dates from 1 November 1958.
*The Dutch coaster **Noord**, discharging at Carr's mill, was built in 1956 and the coal hoist,*
demolished in 1961, is still in situ in the foreground. It is interesting to see the changes at
the mill as evidenced by this photograph and the two on the following page.
(Bernard McCall collection)

The photograph above and that below have been taken from a similar vantage point.
Readers should look carefully at both photographs in order to find any changes.

Sadly the photographs are undated. The most significant change is the extension to Carr's mill.

Associated British Ports - Port of Silloth

General Information

LOCATION

54 deg. 52' N - 03 deg. 24' W. O.S. Grid Reference: NY 105 535.

England, north-west coast. On the S.E. shore of the Solway Firth and is a small sheltered harbour comprising of two docks, the outer of which is tidal, the inner dock is enclosed by dock gates.

Admiralty Charts: 1346 - "Solway Firth and Approaches".
                         2013 - "Saint Bees Head to Silloth".

Admiralty Sailing Directions: NP 37 - "West Coast of England and Wales Pilot".

PORT AUTHORITY

Associated British Ports, Dock Office, Silloth, Cumbria, CA7 4JQ.
Tel. +44 (0)16973-31358. Fax. +44 (0)16873-32709. Email: Silloth@abports.co.uk

The ABP ports of Barrow and Silloth, are jointly administered at Barrow.

Contacts:
Port Manager, ABP North West: Mr Paul Jervis, based at Garston.
Silloth Harbour Master & Port Superintendent: Captain Chris Puxley.

ARRIVAL

ETA and maximum draught should be passed to ship's agent or Harbour Master at least 12 hours before arrival at the pilot station off Workington.

Arrival at the pilot station should be no later that 2 hours before H.W. Silloth in order to catch that tide.

Vessels should endeavour to be loaded/ballasted as near as possible to an even keel on arrival.

Note: H.W. Silloth is approximately 35 minutes after H.W. Liverpool.

ANCHORAGE

Close to the pilot station, located off the port of Workington.

In bad weather from the west or north-west this anchorage can become very exposed and vessels are recommended to seek shelter either in Ramsey Bay, Isle of Man, (34 miles from pilot station), or in Wigtown Bay, S.W. Scotland, (29 miles from pilot station).

Anchorage in the upper reaches of the Solway Firth, i.e. to the north of the 'Solway' buoy, or off Silloth is not recommended except in an emergency, due to the strong flood and ebb tidal currents and the shallows during the low water cycle.

MAX. VESSEL SIZE (New Dock)

Length overall 90m. Beam 13,5m. Draught dependent on tidal height but generally a maximum of 6,5m at Springs and 4,0m at Neaps.
Slightly longer and/or beamier vessels may be accepted at the discretion of the Harbour Master. Limiting factors could be any or all the following: (a) favourable weather conditions, (b) power and manoeuvrability of the vessels, (c) daylight pilotage only, (d) tug assistance, (e) the use of two pilots, (f) available space within the dock.

PILOTAGE

Usually ordered through the Shipping Agency or Harbour Master. Pilotage information updates can be obtained or passed direct via Silloth Dock Office.

Pilotage is compulsory for all vessels of 50m LOA and over, (with certain exceptions).

Pilots for Silloth normally board off the port of Workington at approximately 2 hours before H.W. at Silloth, using the Workington pilot boat. Communications VHF Ch. 14.

Navigation of the upper Solway Firth is not recommended without up-to-date local knowledge. The navigation buoys do not necessarily mark the latest navigable channel. Mariners should exercise extreme caution.

All vessels over 40m LOA inbound for the port of Silloth or the upper reaches of the Solway Firth should report their intentions to 'Silloth Harbour Radio' (VHF Ch. 12) when approaching the 'Solway' buoy or in the vicinity of 54 46N - 03 31W.

Because of the tidal flow across the harbour entrance, vessels can normally only enter Silloth in the period from 30 minutes before H.W., up until H.W. Clearance must be obtained from the Port Authority before entry. The dock gates will normally be opened to allow departure from Silloth during the period from 1.5 hours before H.W., to 1 hour after H.W. Silloth.

PORT DETAILS

Callsign "**Silloth Harbour Radio**" on VHF Ch. 16/12. Listening time 2.5 hours before H.W. to 1 hour after H.W.

The port consists of **Marshall Dock**, a tidal basin, with small craft moorings at the side of a central channel, through which commercial vessels pass via a central channel to reach the working basin of **New Dock**, in which vessels are kept afloat by the use of dock gates. It is in New Dock where the normal commercial activity of the port takes place.

'Marshall Dock' entrance width is 30m, protected on the south side by a short rubble breakwater, marked by 3 timber pile dolphins. The Marshall Dock length is 180m, dock width is 90m. A central channel through 'Marshall Dock' is maintained at a depth below that of the 'New Dock' sill.

'New Dock' entrance width is 16,5 (sill). Dock length is 200m on the south side and 190m on the north side. Dock width is 120m.

'New Dock' entrance contains a pair of hydraulically operated mitre gates.

'New Dock' depth above sill = 7,4m at M.H.W.S. and 5,25m at M.H.W.N.

Quay height is approximately 10m above sill throughout.

There are no tugs based at Silloth, nor are they normally required. Nearest available tug assistance, (to order if required), is at Workington, Barrow or Liverpool.

A copy of the "Port Emergency Plan", along with a copy of local advice and directions for Masters, are placed on board all commercial vessels on arrival. The Emergency Plan is to be returned to the Port Authority immediately prior to departure.

Dock water density approximately 1017-1020.

Fresh water is available at all berths in New Dock.

TIDAL INFORMATION

High Water at Silloth = Approximately 50 minutes after H.W. Dover
35 minutes after H.W. Liverpool
15 minutes after H.W. Workington

Dock Gate Gauge Zero = O.D. Newlyn - 2,6m and C.D./L.A.T. + 1,8m

M.H.W.S. = Gauge Zero + 7,40m   M.H.W.N. =   + 5,25m
Average Quay Height = Gauge Zero + 9,90m

BERTH ALLOCATION (New Dock)

No.1 Berth. Dedicated grain suction discharge facility or layby berth.
No.2 Berth. Molasses discharge facility.
No.3 & 4 Berth. Molasses (CMS) discharge connection/bulk powder loading facility.
No.5 Berth. General cargo/dry bulk loading and discharge quay.
No.6 Berth. As No.5 Berth, plus livestock handling facility.
No.7 Berth. Small ship layby.

STEVEDORE SERVICES

D.A. Harrison, Waverton, Wigton, Cumbria CA7 0AE. Tel. +44 (0)16973-42277.
2 mobile cranes, FLT's, loading shovels, haulage vehicles, storage facilities.
Automatic gravity loading of bulk powders.

STORAGE

There is extensive covered and open storage both within and adjacent to the port.
A cattle/livestock facility lies adjacent to No.6 berth holding up to 600 head.

SHIPPING AGENCY

J. Stronach Ltd, New Dock, Silloth, Cumbria, CA7 4JQ.
Tel. +44 (0)16973-31456.   Fax. +44 (0)16973-32808.

CERTIFICATES, DOCUMENTS

Normal U.K. requirements.

SHIP REPAIRS

Minor repairs can be undertaken by local contractors.

BUNKERS

Bunkers may be ordered through the ship's agent and will be delivered by road tanker.

GARBAGE FACILITIES

Ship's domestic waste may be deposited in special skips located and clearly indicated around the New Dock. Non EU food waste, oily or other waste disposal requirements should be arranged through the ship's agent.

TRADE

Exports - General cargo, bulk powders, bagged fertilisers.

Imports - Bulk grains, bulk and bagged fertilisers, timber products, bulk liquid molasses, general cargo, building materials, livestock.

OTHER INFORMATION

Vessels carrying explosives, or dangerous or hazardous cargo, must declare the fact prior to arrival and comply with relevant Acts, Regulations and Bye-laws.

The landing of all foreign domestic pets is prohibited by UK law.

In bad weather from the west, a swell may be experienced within the port during H.W. cycle, when the dock gates are open. Rubber tyre fendering is placed at intervals around the quay walls.

Vessels must always be ready to move at short notice. Prior permission must be obtained from the Port Authority before disabling main machinery or conducting trials that turn propellers within the dock. Vessels other than small craft must not be left unmanned within the port area.

Diving operations and 'hot work' must not be carried out without a written 'permit' from the Port Authority.

LOCAL INFORMATION

The small town of Silloth, (resident population c. 3000), is located immediately north-east of the port. Within 5 minutes walk from the docks, it has a variety of shops including two small supermarkets, Natwest and HSBC banks, post office, hardware, general goods, hotels, cafes, pubs, social clubs, doctor's surgery, dentists, churches, taxi service, etc. As a small seaside holiday destination, located close to the popular "Lake District" National Park, Silloth is surrounded by caravan parks and holiday accommodation. The population increases significantly through the summer months and during school holidays.

There are local rugby and soccer teams, and squash and tennis courts. A small swimming pool and health club is located within Stanwix Leisure Centre. Silloth-on-Solway Golf Club is located adjacent to the port.

Airports are located at Carlisle (40km), Newcastle (140km) and Manchester (200km).

Regular but infrequent bus services run to Carlisle and Workington.

Nearest railway station is at Wigton (20km), on the Carlisle - Barrow, Cumbrian coastal route.

Nearest mainline railway station is at Carlisle (36km), with links to London, Glasgow, Edinburgh and Newcastle.

Before we look at some modern images of the port, we glance back to a previous era.
This undated photograph is thought to depict a scene from the 1920s or possibly early 1930s.

Arrivals.
The **Sea Eagle** was carrying 2102 tonnes of fertiliser from Beverwijk as she passed fhrough the harbour entrance from the Solway Firth on 4 August 2007.
(Derek McAlone)

The **Scot Explorer** passes through the harbour entrance and into Marshall Dock on 20 May 2007.
She carried a cargo of 1436 tonnes of wood pulp from Antwerp.
(Derek McAlone)

Record breakers.
About to pass through Marshall Dock on 6 July 2008, the **Pur-Navolok** was carrying 3573 tonnes of
bulk fertiliser from Sfax in Tunisia, the fourth largest cargo to have been handled at the port.
(Derek McAlone)

Photographed on 2 April 2007, the **Anmi** was discharging 3901 tonnes of bulk fertiliser from Terneuzen.
At the time, this was the port's biggest cargo of the modern era and is currently
the third biggest in the port's 150-year history.
(Derek McAlone)

We look at two tankers which have delivered cargoes of molasses.
When photographed on 4 February 2007, the **Crescent Connemara** was just arriving
with 2160 tonnes from Bremen.
(Derek McAlone)

The Ukrainian-flagged tanker **Zapadnyy** is the fourth widest to have entered the port. On 14 July 2007
she was preparing to depart after discharging 3023 tonnes of molasses from the Danish port of
Aabenraa, an unusual port of origin for such a cargo.
(Derek McAlone)

Sadly, it is time for farewells.
*The German-owned coaster **Eilsum** departs in July 2005 after delivering wheat from Rostock.*
(Stephen Wright)

*Another German ship, the suitably-named **Navigator**, passes through the harbour entrance on*
20 September 2005 after discharging a cargo of fertiliser from the Polish port of Police.
(Stephen Wright)

SILLOTH ON SOLWAY GOLF CLUB
THE CLUBHOUSE, SILLOTH, WIGTON, CUMBRIA. CA7 4BL

Congratulations to ABP on the 150th anniversary of the opening of Silloth Dock. The Club is pleased to have been associated with the Harbour and surrounding area since 1892.

Play Cumbria's premier championship golf course over the challenging seaside links recently used as the Regional qualifying course for The British Open.

Visitors are welcome to experience the challenge, midweek and at weekends, with a day's golf costing from as little as £40 during the season.

Refurbished Clubhouse available to members and visitors to the Club together with a full catering service.

Why not join the Club to enjoy both the course and clubhouse. Social memberships available from £10 and full playing membership currently costs £340 per year (joining fee applies). Contact the Secretary for full details.

Tel. 016973 31304   email : office@sillothgolfclub.co.uk   www.sillothgolfclub.co.uk

HYDRAULIC & PNEUMATIC ENGINEERING SERVICES

VAT No: 852433336 – Company Reg: 5270715

FOR ALL YOUR HYDRAULIC AND PNEUMATICS NEEDS PLEASE CALL 01900 61100

Hydraulic hose and fittings
Pressure Relief Valve Repair and Recertification
Pressure Gauge Supply and Calibration
Pneumatic and Hydraulic Supplies
Pneumatic and Hydraulic Design and Installation
Pneumatic and Hydraulic Maintenance and Repair
Accumulator Service Overhaul and Recertification
Steel Tube and Fittings
Oil Analysis
Oil Filtration and Filtration Pack Hire
Oil, Degreasants and Detergents Supply
Bespoke Cylinder Manufacture
Hydraulic / Pneumatic Seal Supplies
Pressure Wash Repair and Supplies
Cylinder Repair and Manufacture
Power Pack Manufacture and Hire
Fault Finding and Repair
PTFE and Stainless Steel Convoluted Hoses
Trade Counter
Mobile Breakdown Services

Unit 13, Peart Road, Derwent Howe, Workington, Cumbria, CA14 3YT
Tel: 01900 61100 – Fax: 01900 61177 – Email: derwentfluid@btconnect.com

Kevin Jenkinson – Branch Manager / Sales – 07894 112 089
Jaclyn Carr – Accounts Manager – 01900 61100
Cliff Milligan – Engineer – 07859 894 947
Mike Starkie – Engineer – 07859 894 950
John Harrington – Engineer – 07894 112 101

24 Hour Call Out Please Call 01900 61100

20 March 2007.
*With a snow-topped Criffel dominating the background, the **Antari** makes her approach to the port bringing 3385 tonnes of fertiliser from Ghent. This cargo resulted in a second appearance in the top ten of big cargoes as reported on page 96. She had brought a slightly bigger cargo of fertiliser from IJmuiden in April 2006. We hope that any visitors coming to our port for the 150th anniversary celebrations will, like the **Antari**, make further visits and enjoy Cumbrian scenery and hospitality.*
(Derek McAlone)

Back cover : A fine aerial view of the port with a molasses tanker in port.
(Simon Ledingham)